745.592 Fettig, Hansjürgen
F   Hand and rod puppets; a handbook of
         technique. English version by John Wright
         and Susanne Forster.   Boston, Plays, inc.
         [1974, c1973]
            119 p. illus. 22x29cm.

         Translation of Hand-und Stabpuppen.

         1. Puppet making. I. Title.
jtt   TT174.7.F4713   1974

HAND AND ROD PUPPETS

HAND AND ROD PUPPETS

A Handbook of Technique by Hansjürgen Fettig   English Version by John Wright and Susanne Forster

Boston PLAYS, INC. Publishers

First published in Germany under the title
'Hand- und Stabpuppen'.

First published in the U.S.A. 1973 by Plays, Inc.
8, Arlington Street, Boston, Mass.

© Verlag Frech Stuttgart-Botnang 1970

English translation © George G. Harrap & Co. Ltd 1973

Library of Congress Catalog Card Number: 72-3692
ISBN 0-8238-0140-3

The puppet shown on the back cover of the book was
made by Thomas Franckh under the direction of the
author during an art course at the Schickhardt Gym-
nasium in Stuttgart.
The photograph on page 119 shows a puppet from the
Central Puppet Theatre in Moscow.

Printed in Germany

Foreword

by Ludwig Krafft

The last twenty years have seen a tremendous burst of activity in the field of puppetry, an art usually underestimated by the adult, sceptically watched by the youngster, and adored by the child. Puppetry has now found its way into schools and colleges where it is sometimes used for instructional purposes. Education in road safety, for instance, is now frequently undertaken with the aid of puppet demonstrations. For this particular purpose many towns have started puppet groups which are sent out to visit schools in adjoining areas. Several universities and art colleges have started courses in puppetry and puppet design. Puppet guilds and associations have been formed and there is even an international association for puppeteers. Puppet museums and institutes for studying and maintaining puppet traditions have opened, and all over the world puppet festivals, supported by international puppeteers, are being held. Many thousands are spent on the furtherance of puppetry, although this regrettably is not entirely true of conditions in Germany and England.

At teachers' colleges in Germany puppetry has become a part of the curriculum, and all nursery and kindergarten teachers have to study it as a subject. Puppetry has also found its way into hospitals and mental homes where it is used therapeutically with otherwise unapproachable patients, and often helps to re-integrate people into society. At any school the occasional puppet performance brings general excitement and provides useful relaxation in strenuous weeks of study.

One knows that the puppet theatre is an ideal counter attraction to the crime-laden detective story and the shattering sensationalism of the Wild West film. With their atmosphere of suspense, these dubious forms of entertainment can be said to help to release children from their inhibitions; but in the end they cannot compete with the puppets. When the puppet show is over there are no corpses to trouble the young imagination, there are only wooden villains who have been punished for their misdeeds by the popular puppet heroes of the fairground tradition.

Many institutions, youth clubs, religious and social organisations include puppet shows in their festivities, and although the quality of the performances given by the amateur or professional may vary considerably, I do not think it is an exaggeration to say that puppetry has become indispensable on such occasions.

There is no doubt that puppetry is, to an increasing degree, capturing the imagination of art teachers and their pupils who sometimes work voluntarily outside school hours on the school's puppet stage. It is the teachers of art, music and literature who can give the young people an opportunity, not provided in any other section of the curriculum, to explore their own creative abilities through the medium of puppetry. And as puppetry does not end in the workshop, but continues with the actual theatrical presentation, it can well be regarded as a very effective vehicle for discovering and developing artistic talent which would otherwise remain dormant in a child. By comparison, the traditional practice of making children recite poetry in a classroom provides far less stimulus.

Work with puppetry has never failed to awaken in young people interest and talent which helps to form their personalities in later life. Biographies of artists often bear witness to the stimulating effect of puppetry during childhood, an effect never quite forgotten. And it is not only those who practice in the artistic professions who profit from these activities at school, but also those who are involved in the 'social' professions such as teachers or psychologists.

As interest in puppetry grows, questions on how to make, manipulate and stage puppets multiply. Which is the best material to use for making puppets? How does a puppet have to be constructed in order to be able

c. 2

to perform certain tasks? What are the technical tricks one has to know in order to construct a puppet with the maximum elegance or grotesqueness of movement when animated? It is, of course, marvellous when a group of devoted people try to find their own way of solving problems, but this way of going about things often wastes time and causes frustration, as beginners are usually unable to cope with a project that is too advanced. It includes unnecessary detours and failures which might well prove discouraging if they outnumber successful results. Therefore, one looks to handbooks for assistance. Unfortunately some of these books are written by people who have never made a puppet technically good enough to appear on a stage. Their instructions for making puppets vaguely hint at 'old pieces of material', 'wood', 'cardboard', and 'glue' and are only good for people who wish to indulge in an idle pastime; they do not inspire creative theatrical production. Puppets made as crudely as suggested in some of these books have no presence or 'personality', and it is not surprising that many of them end up in a dusty corner rather than being used for any creative purpose.

It is, therefore, high time that this excellent handbook on puppet making should appear on the market, especially as it deals predominantly with rod puppets, in our time a highly favoured type of puppet. In its construction the rod puppet combines elements of both glove and string puppets. The rod puppet's ancestors still perform in the Far East, Japan, China and Indonesia portraying the gods and god-like emperors and heroes of the local legends. The same method of manipulation was used by the wandering performers of nativity plays in Austria and Eastern Europe. Their puppets have long since become exhibition pieces in museums. Only in Cologne and Aachen have the old rod puppets actively survived.

After the Second World War the rod puppet became a most favoured medium, but its conquest of the Western World is not yet ended. Therefore it is well worth while to investigate the manifold mechanical possibilities of this highly versatile type of puppet, and to study its variety of movement. Only a few puppeteers have dared experiment with the rod puppet so far, but they have, I understand, always achieved great success.

This book reveals innumerable examples of practical experiments in making and manipulating glove and rod puppets of all types. The author, who works not only as a painter and puppet maker but also as an art teacher, very generously makes his knowledge available to his readers, according to the belief that there is no secret in puppetry except its fascination for the puppeteer.

Contents

Introduction

I do not think we would be wrong to assume that a particularly well-shaped stone, a peculiar piece of branch or root, or a carved stick served the prehistoric child as a doll, in which case we may say that the doll is probably as old as mankind.

When we remember our own childhood or watch children at play with dolls, we realise that a doll fills the role of a child's child, or at least a child's friend. A child treats a doll as a living creature that listens and answers and is either good or bad. All this happens in spite of the fact that the child is fully aware that a doll is nothing but a toy.

Now if the doll, which is a static creature, can generate such strong feeling, we can well imagine what a great impact an animated puppet has on a child. When we watch an audience of children at a puppet performance, we can observe how vigorously they support the good characters and oppose the bad ones, even to the point of tears and shouts of hatred.

This demonstrates how young children are almost completely at the mercy of their environment, and the way in which it is interpreted to them by their parents, their nursery school teachers, their instructors and their friends and of course also by puppeteers behind the scenes who present shows to them. The medical and biological sciences tell us that a major part of a person's character is formed by education.

Heritage and education develop the characteristics that make a person. These are reflected in the expression of his face and are revealed by his hands and in fact by his whole body with its rhythm of movement. This explains the two objectives I have in writing this book and has much to do with my attitude towards puppetry in general.

There are currently two opposing principal opinions on modern puppetry and both are valid. Everyone who takes up puppetry must decide whether he will follow the emotional romantic realistic school or whether he will be more interested in abstract construction and the so-called art for art's sake attitude. The former means a continuation of the old puppet tradition, taking into account, of course, new educational principles. The latter follows the school of thought of Wasily Kandinsky, Oskar Schlemmer, the Bauhaus, constructive art, and Op and Pop art, all of which aim at a more abstract and formal artistic representation.

I personally care little as to whether I am classified as antiquated or modern in my ideas about puppetry, but while I have nothing against the abstract school, I must say straight away that I feel more at home with the romantic realism of the old puppet tradition. I am interested in man and his appearance in his environment. Sympathy and a critical eye are necessary for this study. I see the puppet as a caricature of man, as stylised reality. Elements of realism, expressionism, symbolism, fairy tale and caricature combine to make this kind of puppet. Rightly understood this puppet is not an imitation, but a symbol of man. Convincing and alive it takes man's place, yet must follow the laws of art.

And now having stated my views I must hasten to point out to my readers that not all of the information contained in this book is of my own invention. Be that as it may I feel that I should here and now express my gratitude to those who have helped in many ways, not all of whom I am able to mention here. I want to express my special gratitude to Kurt Selin of the firm of Braun booksellers in Heidelberg who first introduced me to the puppet world. Also to the late Theodor Schück of Freiburg/Breisgau, who was my art teacher and whose puppet theatre at school inspired me to take up puppetry. Also to the lecturer Hans Amann and to the late Professor Paul Thesing who taught at the Lehrwerkstätten für Bildende Kunst at Darmstadt, and to Dr. H. R. Purschke publisher of the specialist's magazine 'Perlicko — Perlacko' in Frankfurt. Special thanks are due to Ludwig Krafft, the founder and director of the Munich Puppet Museum, and last but not least to Herr Krauss of Frech Verlag in Stuttgart-Botnang, who kindly and generously promoted the publication of this book.

The numbers in brackets in the text refer to the drawings which illustrate the problems under discussion.

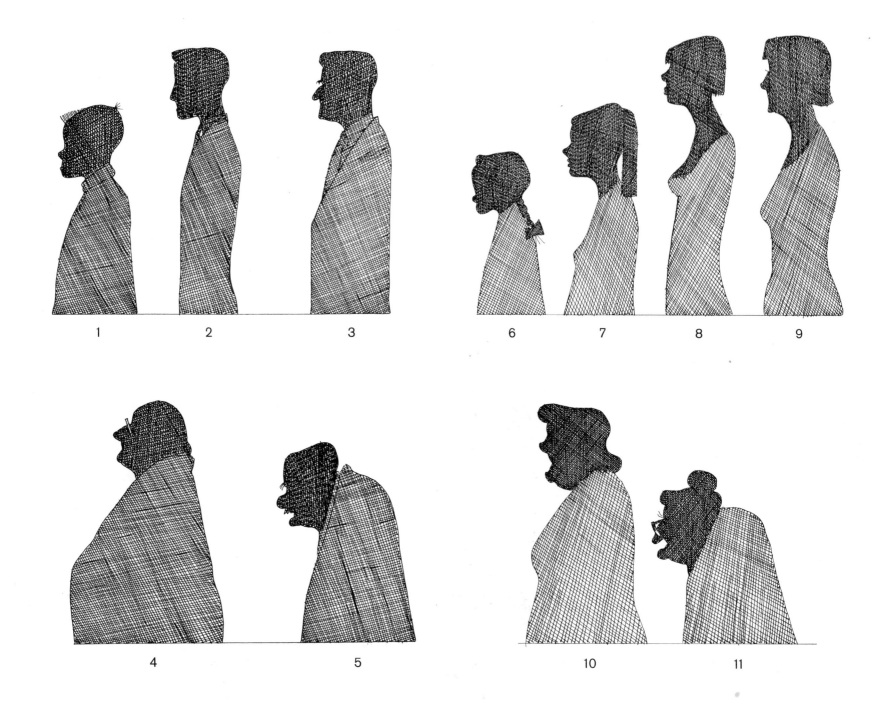

1   2   3

6   7   8   9

4   5

10   11

10

CHAPTER I People

a) General appearance:

Before starting to construct puppets it is necessary to make a study of the essential characteristics of different types of human beings. According to Kretschmer's typology[1] there are three major categories:
1. 'Pyknik', the small tubby type.
2. 'Athletik', the medium-size slim and muscular type.
3. 'Leptosom', the tall skinny, thin-boned type.

There are, of course, a great number of variations and permutations of these types, but for the purpose of this book it might be as well to keep to the above simplified classification.

'Pykniker', the small tubby type is shrewd, witty and sometimes unexpectedly nimble. He perspires and gets out of breath and is usually good-natured but sometimes hot tempered. In a puppet ensemble such a type could play the part of a simple comedian — one who enjoys life.

'Athletiker', is medium-sized and strong, quick, exact and dashing. He walks upright, is proud and confident, clever with his hands, but not very bright. He can be good-natured or brutal. Here we have the stock figure for the bullying hero, robber, policeman, craftsman, worker, or playboy on our puppet stage.

'Leptosome', the tall, thin-boned type, stiff

[1] Koerperbau und Charakter, Dr. H. C. Ernst Kretschmer, Springer Verlag 1931, latest edition 1955.

or doubled up, is intelligent, noble or treacherous, or fragile and perpetually peevish. He can be mean, haughty or cowardly. His scheming creates confusion and suspense, but more often than not the 'Pykniker' gets the better of him in the end. The tall, thin type can, of course, make the ideal counterpart to the small and tubby.

All three types, however different, are constructed according to the same laws of proportion. Let us demonstrate this by way of a little experiment: touch your chin with the wrist of one of your hands and stretch it over your face. You will find that the tip of your middle-finger reaches, approximately, to the centre of your forehead, and that the hand almost covers the whole face. The puppet hand should be in the same proportion as this to the puppet head, or may sometimes be even bigger. Now bend your left arm to a right angle and place your right hand straight against the inside of the lower arm. You will find that hand and lower arm are of the same length. The same applies to the upper arm. Now stand up and let your arms hang down. Your middle finger touches your thigh halfway down. This remains true whatever your size, small or tall, slender or fat.

Fig. 25 shows a profile divided into three equal sections. The ear is in the centre of the middle section starting exactly at the back end of the lower jaw. This profile is well proportioned and might be considered beautiful, but it is not very interesting. Perfect harmony of proportion does not necessarily make a puppet face beautiful and can even be boring.

But before discussing further the particular nature of puppets, let us look at figs. 1 to 11. These show a series of realistic silhouettes illustrating the general development of a man and a woman from childhood to old age. If dress and hairstyle were to be exchanged granny could easily be turned into grandpa or vice versa (5 and 11), similarly with the girl and the boy (1 and 6). The difference of the sexes becomes apparent, however, during the time of puberty and maturity. Study the body-shapes and the general deportment and observe how the profile gets more and more pointed as age increases. Look at the slender neck of the child and the well developed back of its head, its round forehead and the chubby, even bulging mouth and chin. Now compare the children to the grandparents who seem to have almost entirely lost their necks, and whose lean mouths and chins reveal their toothlessness. Observe the people you meet and conscientiously study their characteristics. To make convincing puppets we need this knowledge of people.

Although we may not wish to make small exact replicas, we need this knowledge of people's characteristics for reference. In this way we can find the right measure of exaggeration or understatement essential to the design (or make up) of a good puppet.

b) Variations within the general rule:

If a puppet is convincing and alive, its character, degree of intelligence and emotional state will be evident, also its age and background should be apparent. Therefore you should train your sense of observation. Observation means conscious watching; you must be able to describe in terms of puppetry exactly what you have seen.

Figs. 12 to 24 show a number of profiles which are very different from one another. They are shown in pairs to make the difference as obvious as possible. Although we can only show a small percentage of the innumerable possibilities of human faces, it becomes evident how very different they can be from the scheme of proportions mentioned earlier (fig. 25).

If you are willing to go through the following exercises, you will find them a great help when you want to invent your own puppets.

1. Try to write down the characteristics of the profiles 12-24 and describe how the pairs differ from each other. For instance fig. 12, left profile:

– well-fed, 45 to 50 years old, normal high forehead slanting slightly backwards, forehead and nose clearly separated by a dip, big strong rather distinct hook nose, drooping lower lip that is slightly displaced in relation to the upper lip, underdeveloped round chin slightly receding. It is mainly the nose, the strong forehead and the fleshy somewhat sagging cheeks that define the face. As far as it is at all possible to determine a person's profession from his face, this gentleman could own a store or work as a civil servant. He is of moderate temperament, without exceptional characteristics. In comparison the profile opposite seems to belong to a gentleman with more intelligence and energy. We gain this impression from the exceptionally high fore-

head and the small yet pronounced chin. The tautness of the profile is also a sign of energy, with its small, protruding, slightly bent nose and its straight, thin lower lip which slants inwards a little before reaching the chin. This gentleman could be a doctor or a lawyer. Like the character represented by the profile opposite him he is also about 50 years old.

It would be a profitable exercise for you, if you studied the other profiles in this manner, and tried to find similar characteristics in the faces you meet in the street, at work, and amongst your friends.

2. Try to give these profiles (or others you have invented) suitable head shapes, hair and headgear.

3. When you have completed exercise 2 try to give the heads suitable bodies, in outline only as in figs. 1 to 11. (This exercise could also be executed in black paper cutouts instead of outlines.) It is important to concentrate on the essential characteristics, not on ornamental details.

4. Please note that none of the profiles in figs. 12 to 24 are showing any particular emotional state. The facial muscles are in a relaxed position from which laughter, crying, pain, surprise, anger or benevolence can develop, not to mention of course silence and shouting. We must take the fact fully into account that the puppet head has neither muscles nor skin and therefore has no possibility of altering its facial expression. Once made, the face remains as it is and a laughing face, can never look sad, a screaming face never silent. The older a person becomes, the easier it is to determine his basic

attitudes and characteristics from his face even when he is relaxed. This is also true of his general deportment, and it is important to note whether he walks upright or bent, whether he is leaning forward or backward, whether his neck is stretched or slack, and whether he pulls his stomach in or pushes it out.

5. Now try to find out why I have ascribed certain characteristics to the following profiles (in each diagram I refer to the left profile as a and the right as b)-

13 b: Attentive, determined, strong-willed.

15 b: Perpetually discontented, peevish.

19 b: Good-natured, benevolent, not too difficult to influence, yet not stupid.

20 a: Contemplative, wise, gentle, yet strong-willed.

20 b: Downhearted, pensive, understanding.

21 b: Good-natured and simple-minded, but in the event of provocation possibly irascible.

22 a: Haughty, just misses being genteel, taciturn.

23 b: Intelligent bully, bright person with strong will power. He could be a leading engineer on a building site.

Such exercises should be practiced and extended. They are of essential value in the making of good puppets.

c) Differences between humans and puppets?

A human being has about 500 or 600 different muscles giving movement to his body and face. The skin has great flexibility. Yet the glove-puppet head, to take an example,

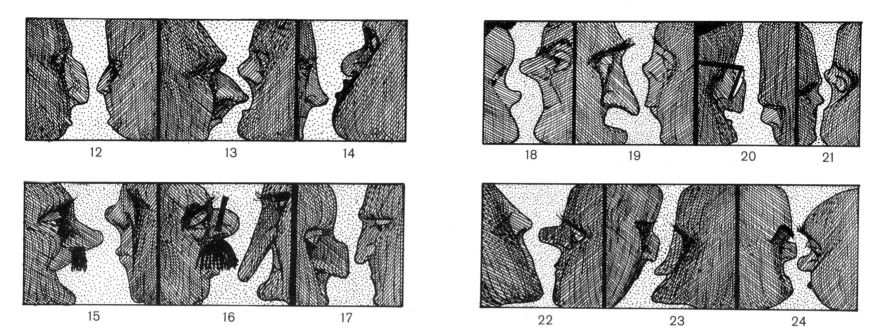

12   13   14   18   19   20   21

15   16   17   22   23   24

is made of wood or other inflexible substances and has one fixed expression. Its body is a fabric bag which may serve as costume as well as glove for the puppeteer's hand and arm, and usually only three fingers are used for manipulating the glove puppet. The movement of those three fingers plus the movement of the manipulator's wrist and arm symbolise the functions of the 500 to 600 muscles in the human body. With the rod-puppet the possibility of movement is increased by mechanical devices built into the body. No matter how intricate this mechanism may be, however, there is no hope of ever imitating even remotely the interplay of 500 to 600 muscles. So we see that it would be clearly absurd to plan a puppet as a replica of man. Any attempt at naturalism invariably leads to an inartistic result. Only

if the puppeteer succeeds in conceiving a puppet that mechanically and visually is a plausible symbol of a certain type of person, and only if this puppet is well operated, does the audience accept the puppet as a 'living' creature.

A puppet cannot move alone; it has to be supported and moved by a puppeteer. It is essential, therefore, that a puppet should fit in with the physical proportions of whoever is handling it, and it should be designed so that the most can be made of the physical circumstances of its operation. Glove or rod puppets should not be smaller than 30 cm and not much taller than 60 cm. If they are less than 30 cm, they will be too small to be seen properly. If they are taller than 60 cm they may be too heavy to carry and will hardly fit the proportions of a normal puppet

booth or stage. Therefore the height of the puppet-head should range between 10 to 20 cm. With this rough idea of proportionate size in mind, you can easily imagine how little of a puppet can be seen from a 15 to 20 metres distance, and it follows that the features and movements of any puppet should be as simple and definite as possible and their mechanisation planned accordingly.

To summarise all we have dealt with so far let us say that the puppet is a simple, and at the same time, artistic symbol of a person, and that its success depends upon its particular adaptation to the available possibilities of basic movement, and how powerfully its characteristics are conveyed.

13

CHAPTER II

Basic Design

The mechanical side of manipulation will be dealt with in a later chapter. For the moment let us look at figs. 25 and 26 which attempt to show the difference between puppets and people.

Fig. 25 shows a simplified drawing of the head of a man between 20 and 25 years of age. The horizontal lines cut the head into three equal sections: forehead — eyes, nose and ears — mouth and chin. The dotted line at the top marks the skull and shows how the hair rises above it, thus rendering the shape of the head irregular and, as it were more interesting. Yet, because of its complete symmetry, this head lacks personal expression and is rather unappealing. This pattern is important, however, because it helps to check measurements when we use exaggeration as a means of creating a caricature. It is in the nature of caricature to alter these standard proportions. If one of the three sections is increased at the cost of the others a more original and therefore a more interesting face is the result.

In fig. 26 we see a simplified version of the same nondescript character. To make such a head, start with a wooden darner (lathe-turned egg) upside down. Make the neck from 10 or 12 mm hardwood dowel glued into a hole drilled at a certain angle. The matter of determining this angle is dealt with in a later paragraph. Make the nose in the form of a rounded off wooden wedge fastened to the head with the aid of a wooden plug and glue. The wig could be made of raffia, wool, felt or leather and then fixed to the head. (The same method could be applied when making the heads shown in figs. 51 to 73.)

The correct relative angle of the head of the puppet to the audience is of the greatest importance and fig. 27 shows how this angle can be ascertained.

Generally the eye level of the audience is 120 cm above floor level. The height of the glove or rod puppet playboard is determined by the height of the tallest puppeteer in the group, and this is generally about 180 cm, so that if the puppets are between 30 and 40 cm, the difference between the puppets' eye level and the audience's eye level is about 100 cm. If there is a fair distance between audience and puppets this need not be a serious matter, but if, as is so often the case, the first row should be only 3 m from the booth, the impression is that the puppet looks above the heads of the audience instead of at them.

When discussing the modelling of heads, many puppet handbooks recommend the use of a modelling stand (fig. 28). Do not use it, it is much better to work without it.

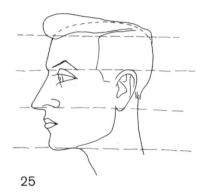

25

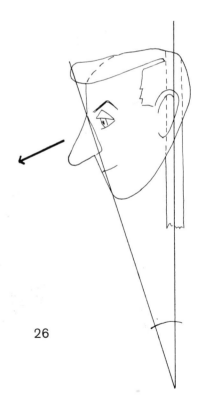

26

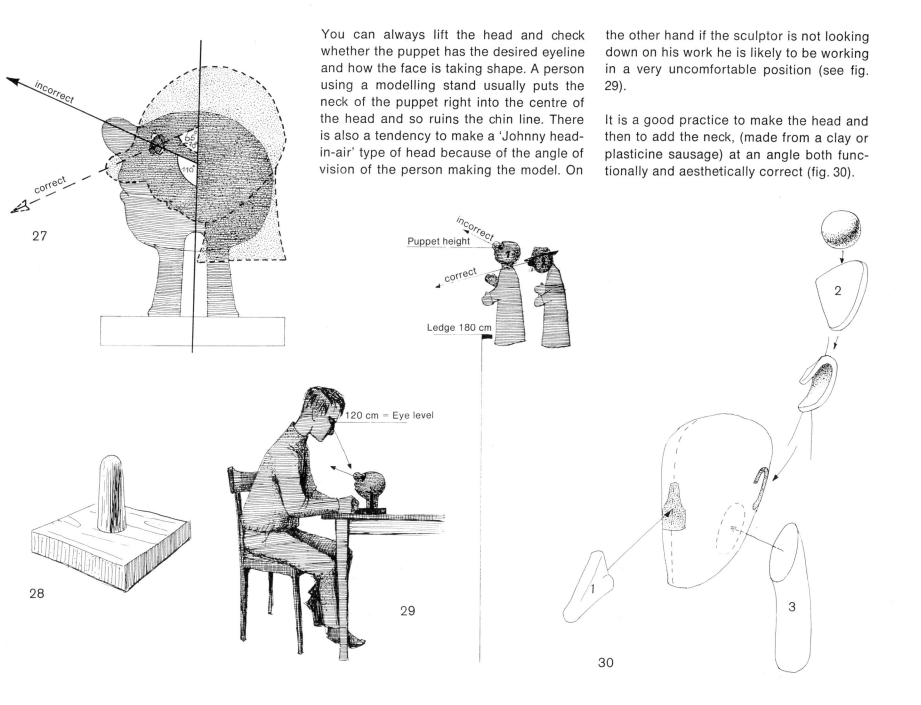

You can always lift the head and check whether the puppet has the desired eyeline and how the face is taking shape. A person using a modelling stand usually puts the neck of the puppet right into the centre of the head and so ruins the chin line. There is also a tendency to make a 'Johnny head-in-air' type of head because of the angle of vision of the person making the model. On the other hand if the sculptor is not looking down on his work he is likely to be working in a very uncomfortable position (see fig. 29).

It is a good practice to make the head and then to add the neck, (made from a clay or plasticine sausage) at an angle both functionally and aesthetically correct (fig. 30).

incorrect

correct

27

28

Puppet height

incorrect

correct

Ledge 180 cm

120 cm = Eye level

29

30

1

2

3

15

31

32

33

34

35

36

37

16

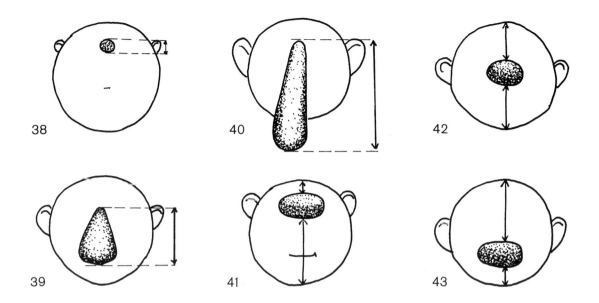

38   40   42

39   41   43

The three examples in figs. 31 to 37 show how the design of expressive puppet heads can be derived from realistic human portraits.

By enlarging chin and nose (compare figs. 31, 32 and 33) the face becomes more brutal in expression. If you compare fig. 31 with 33, you will see quite clearly the difference in proportion. The strong-willed, not altogether pleasant expression in 31 has become brutal in 33.

The intermediate stages are not shown in examples 34 and 36. In both cases the upper skull and forehead have been enlarged, the shapes and lines of the faces have become more definite and angular, and the noses more prominent. Also the contrast of light and shade has been intensified, thus emphasising eyes and hair. The mouth has been

reduced to an unobtrusive line. The chin in fig 35. sticks out at a sharper angle than in 34. The eyes in 35 are more deep set than in 34, thus creating an interesting play of light and shade, which can be used to show a change of facial expression.

In principle the human head can be said to be egg-shaped. An egg can be defined as a misshapen ball, but as the ball is the simpler shape of the two let us start with that.

Apart from the shape of the head, the nose is the most important feature of a puppet face. The nose can have all shapes and sizes and it can be placed in three different positions on the face. It can be either in its normal position in the centre of the face (39/42), or it can be lower or higher than the centre. In 38 and 41 the lower part of the face is unnaturally enlarged at the cost of the

forehead, and in 43 the reverse is the case. It is said that silly people have small brains. Therefore the puppet face on which the nose sits higher than usual generally belongs to a foolish character. Similarly a strong chin is seen as a sign of energy, an abnormally strong chin as that of brutality. This is quite often true and we can accept these generalisations for most purposes. So as you work bear in mind all that can be achieved by using this play of proportion in combination with the simple variations from the basic shape, say, of the ball.

But before we go on let us quickly examine fig. 40. Here the base of the nose is in its normal position, but the nose itself is excessively long. When such a head is manipulated, the nose looks like the hand of a clock and the effect is very funny.

Figs. 44 to 49 show the simplest deviations from the shape of a ball. Each of these variations is used subsequently for several simple puppet head designs, as shown in figs. 50 to 76.

These basic shapes for the heads can be of wood turned in a lathe, or they can be made with the aid of a stocking, stuffed, or from fabric, fruit, or vegetables, or, of course by covering models with paper or sacking and glue (this technique is discussed in the next chapter). For making hair, spectacles and general accessories for the head, you need raffia, cord, wool, wire, felt, moss, saucepan cleaners, cigar holders, buttons and so on. There is practically no limit to what you can use. Real hair, by the way, is one of the few things not recommended.

18

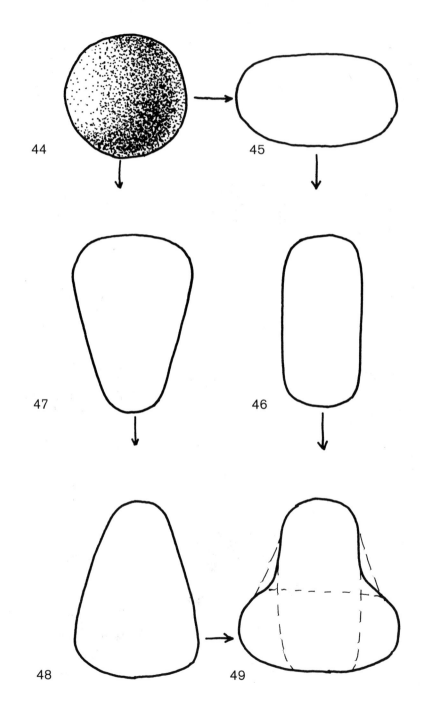

44

45

47

46

48

49

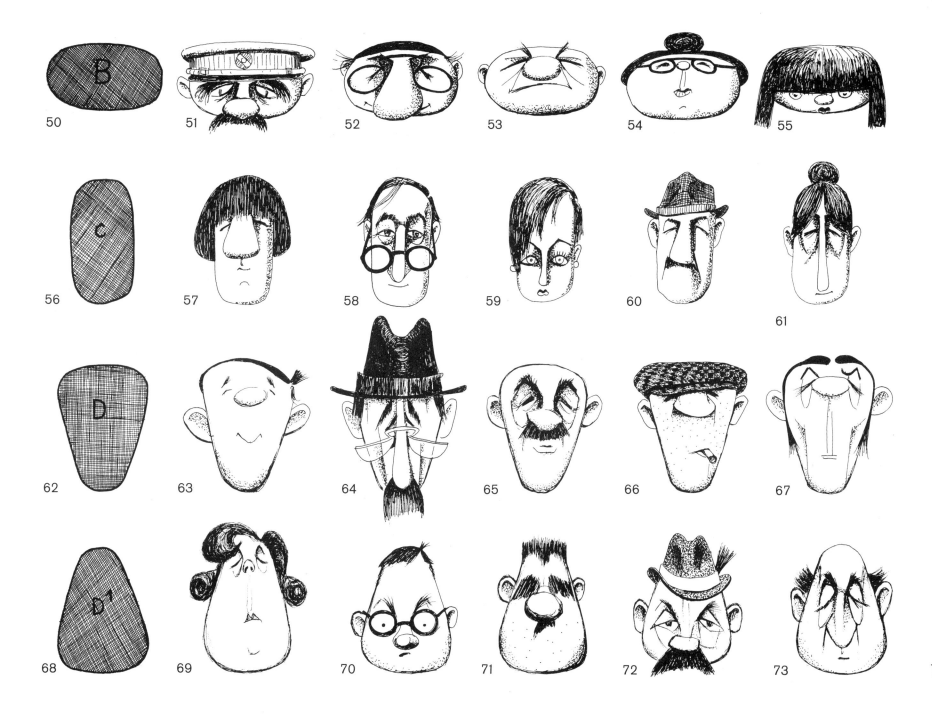

50

51

52

53

54

55

56

57

58

59

60

61

62

63

64

65

66

67

68

69

70

71

72

73

19

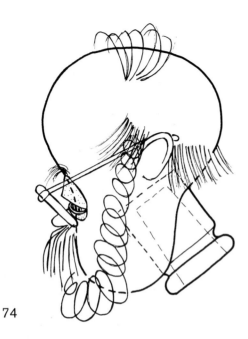

74

75

76

If you want to make a set of puppets quickly, a good way to do this is to turn the heads in a lathe. Figs. 74 to 78 suggest a number of possible shapes. The more you vary the shapes of the heads, the more interesting your group of puppets will be. As a general rule it is recommended that you give character to the turned shape by adding nose, hair, eyes, or a pipe or a pair of glasses rather than by changing the shape with file and sandpaper. Figs. 77 and 78 illustrate my meaning. If you look at 77 and pretend that nose, eyes and mouth were not there, all you would notice would be the fat neck-line. Seen from the front, the big bulging middle section of head 77 represents the cheeks, and seen from the side as in fig. 78, cheeks and neck at the same time. As I do not wish to cramp the reader's imagination by an over-abund-ance of material I shall illustrate this theme with only three examples.

It is not within the scope of this book to explain the techniques of wood turning. If you wish to use a lathe you will of course obtain the necessary machine and you will undoubtedly find some literature which will explain how it should be handled. Even a beginner should be able to turn numerous simple shapes after he has done a few preliminary exercises.

As puppets made of vegetables and fruit usually do not last for very long, it is enough to wrap a piece of cloth around the puppeteer's hand, and push the upper part of the cloth into the hole at the neck with the index finger. You can use small onions for eyes.

For pupils you can use pins, which also hold the eyes in place. The nose can be a little radish, and hair asparagus, twigs, parsley or corn leaves. These are only suggestions, of course. On stage these puppets are particularly good in violent robber scenes. An audience will cry with laughter when the antagonists actually hack each other to pieces, or when a quack doctor performs organ transplantations.

As a last example of a simple puppet, I want to mention the Attorney-General in fig. 80, a puppet made of cloth with a stuffed stocking head. His glasses are made of wire wound with black raffia. The hollow cheeks are formed by taking in the stocking in the appropriate places. The nose is made from different coloured cloth, stuffed and sewn to the face.

20

77

78

79

80

21

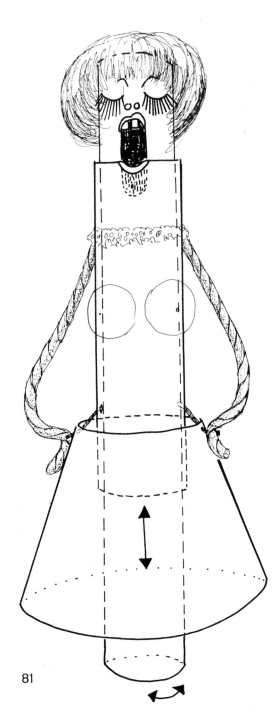

A totally different type of puppet is shown in fig. 81. Annie Weigand, directing a group of puppeteers from a youth club in Stuttgart and using puppets made in this way, was internationally successful. Two cardboard tubes of slightly different diameter and with one sliding inside the other represent the head and body. Skirt and mobile hips are made from a truncated cone fastened to the outer tube with two pieces of string. A wavy wig, made of wool, raffia, feathers or paper, blue eyelids and huge eyelashes, and two pieces of rope for arms complete this pop singer. The mouth, a hole cut out of the inner tube, is operated by pushing the inner tube up and down and twisting it sideways; the operator can thus get any visual variation from whispering to shouting. An organ grinder and his wife were made the same way so was a whole company of singers. The conductor was represented by a simple tube placed on the head of the operator who used his own hand in a white glove for holding the baton and conducting.

The audience was delighted and called for one encore after another. This sort of performance, which does not require a great amount of preparation, is ideal for school festivities or for an evening of light entertainment in a youth club. If these simple techniques are employed and a workshop is well organised, the puppets for a full evening's programme can be made by a group of people in a single afternoon. Select a few witty records, use an off-key choir, an old tinny soprano and a pompous, continually fluffing orator etc., and you can be sure the evening will be a success, with the simple puppets mentioned above.

In spite of the very excellent results obtainable with these puppets we should bear in mind that they have one great weakness and that is that they can only perform in one act and such an act should not last much longer than two or three minutes. They can excel in that one number, but can not do much else. An ingenious person could devise one or even two successful programmes with these one-act puppets, but after that they would have to repeat themselves and the acts would become less and less effective. Figs. 82 to 88 demonstrate various ways of using cardboard tubes for making puppets. The skilful use of the keyhole saw or, better still, the mitre-saw, is essential for this technique.

The drawings, I think, are self-explanatory. For constructing the heads you should follow a certain procedure:

1. Saw the tubing diagonally across.

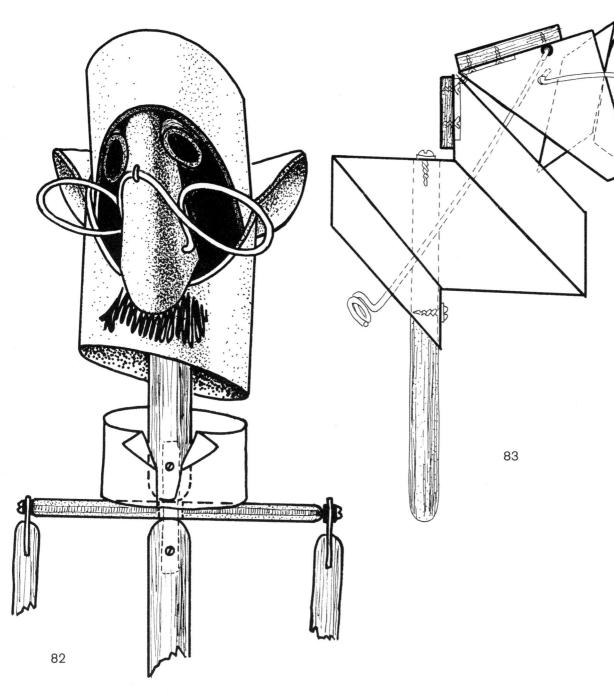

82

83

2. Glue single pieces together at an appropriate angle, or connect them with hinges, or push one part into the other and then glue them together.

3. Noses, eyes and ears should be cut from thinner tubing in the same fashion and added to the face.

4. Spectacles, hair, etc., can then be added.

5. The mechanical gadgets for the movement and the control should be made with a hardwood dowel, hinges and screws.

6. When all this is done you can start to dress the puppet.

The mouths of the teacher (fig. 82) and the caretaker (fig. 86) are covered by beards. The teacher's beard is firmly glued to the face, the caretaker's is only partly stuck to it and therefore has a certain amount of free movement; his cap makes the tubular construction of his head less apparent. Granny's hairstyle (figs. 83-85) has the same effect. Contrary to nature, granny's lower jaw does not move, but her upper face does and this reversal of facial movement makes her funny. Grandpa's lower jaw, however, is mobile; it has a string-joint and is moved by the index finger of the operator.

84

85

86

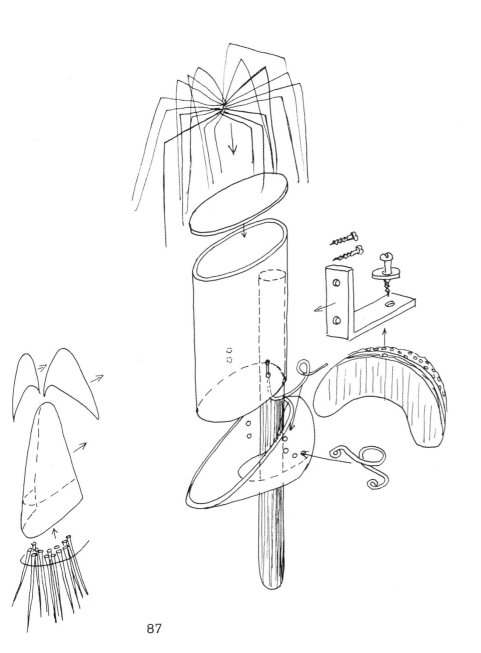

87

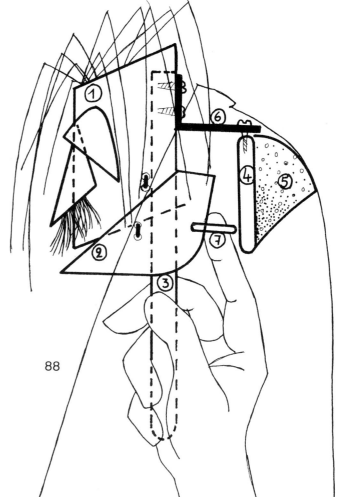

88

The encircled numbers in fig. 88 indicate:
1. and 2. The head and lower jaw made from cardboard tubing.
3. A hardwood dowel for holding the puppet.
4. The shoulder piece made of plywood.
5. Foam-rubber padding.
6. An iron bracket with three holes to which head, shoulders and main rod are fixed. It also serves as a joint for the shoulder-piece.

To the materials we have been discussing so far (wood, vegetables, stuffed stockings, cardboard tubing) we could add any packaging material such as plastic bottles or cardboard boxes. These have their own finished shape which we can use and decorate as our imagination dictates. If we don't use it in its manufactured shape we must nevertheless treat each material in accordance with its specific properties. It would be absurd, for instance, to soak cardboard tubing in water till it can be modelled. If you want to model, use the materials that best lend themselves to this task such as clay or plasticine. You can either cover the finished model with paper, sacking and glue (as described in the following chapter), and subsequently scoop the clay or plasticine out, or you can make a negative plaster mould of it and then cast a positive one.

Ordinary clay has an unfortunate way of drying out and shrinking, and apart from the fact of having to knead it and keep it moist, it is a dirty material to use for puppet-making purpose, and therefore not ideal.
Good plasticine keeps its plasticity for decades and can be used at any time without preparation. It is so easy to shape, however, that an amateur could be misled into using it for unnecessarily elaborate decoration and detail, thus detracting from the power of expression of a face or even killing it completely. To include meticulous detail of facial expression such as superfluous wrinkles and warts usually leads to unconvincing and tasteless results. Therefore always aim for a clear, simple, uncomplicated shape.

26

By en larging each square in the grate grad to 10 × 10 mm one will obtain the truc true sice

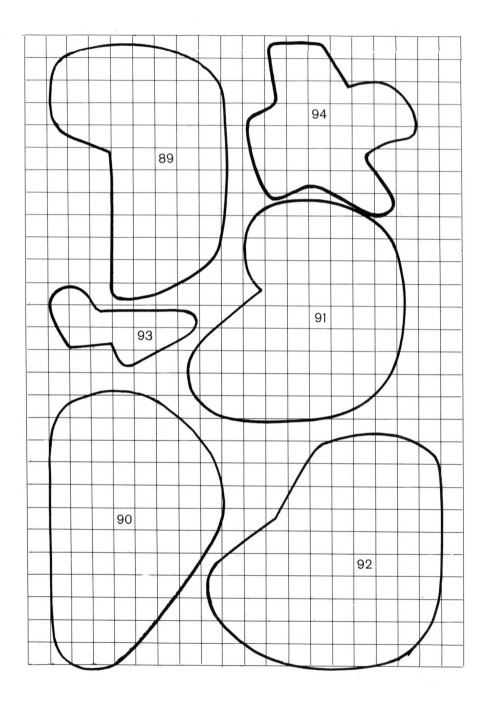

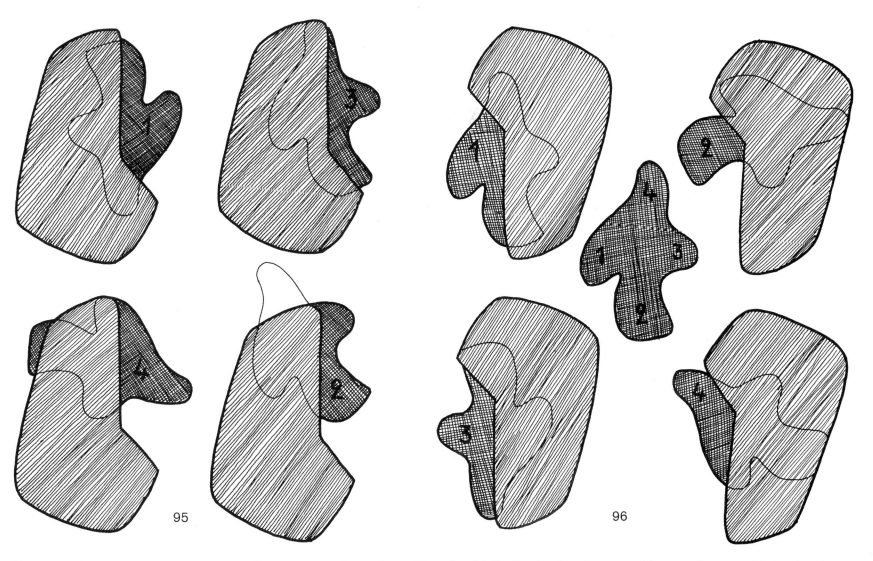

95

96

How to arrive at it is demonstrated in figs. 89 to 104.

The patterns shown here are made from strong brown paper. If you play around with them, put them on top of each other, slide and shift them about and exchange their position, you will get a great deal of inspiration from them. You should fix the best results with glue and add hats, caps, glasses, beards, hair, cigars, pipes etc.

Your three dimensional plasticine heads should look as clear and simple from every side as these flat paper profiles.

Figs. 97 to 100 show four heads with a fam-

ily resemblance; they could be brothers and sisters. Small variations give each one a distinct individual character.

Figs. 101 to 104 show four complete puppet designs. Here you can see again how clarity and simplicity of shape account for their strength of expression.

27

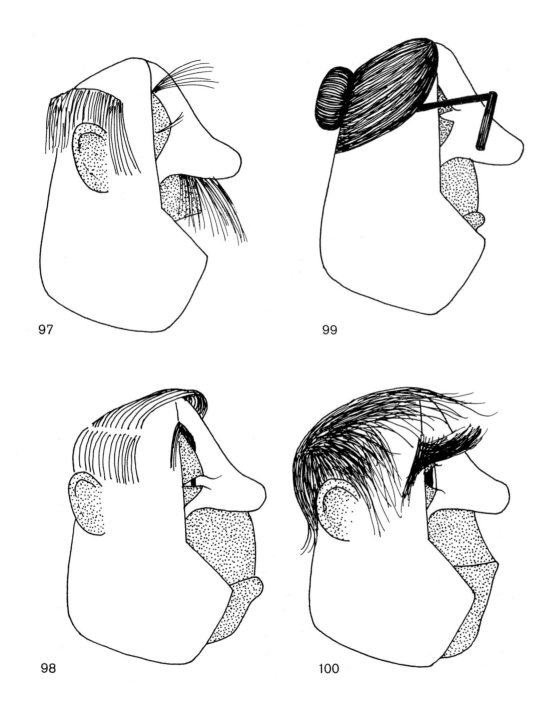

97

99

28   98

100

101

102

103

104

29

CHAPTER III

Basic Techniques

How to model with paper and glue:

This technique has always been used in theatre workshops because it is cheap and quick, and the results are hard-wearing. In this way huge statues, masks, expensive looking props and so on can be made most satisfactorily. For making puppets it is ideal. At little cost you can make any shape and it will be strong, hollow and light. Here is a list of materials and tools needed:

1. 2.5 kg plasticine (this is enough for a normal puppet head).
2. 125 gm of cellulose wall-paper paste.
3. One tube of contact adhesive.
4. One tube of Bostik glue.
5. Strong paper in at least two colours.
6. Hessian or sacking, and old pieces of cloth.
7. Scotch glue (the type known as pearl glue).
8. A glue-pot.
9. Brushes for Scotch glue and paste.
10. An old table-knife with a round top, or a spoon-shaped steel spatula for modelling.
11. A sharp, pointed knife.
12. A strong, sharp pair of scissors.

As listed above, you need about 2.5 kg of plasticine. This is oil-processed clay, always ready for use, but a bit hard when cold. Normal room temperature renders it just right for modelling. If while you work it should get too warm and soft in your hands, you can control its consistency by dipping it into cold water. After the paper mould over the plasticine model is finished and dried, the plasticine is removed and is ready to be used again. Plasticine is generally available in art material shops and toy shops.

Working procedure

When making a head with layers of paper and glue add water to the wall-paper paste powder as described on the packet. After the recommended time of setting stir more cold water into the paste till it drops thickly from your brush. For our purposes the paste should be slightly thinner than would be required for wall-papering. But at the same time it should not be too watery.

Next you tear from your sheet of strong paper large, irregular pieces (3 to 5 times as big as your hands). Make sure there are no cut edges, as these would eventually show clearly on the puppet head. Put the pieces on a non-absorbent surface and paint them on both sides with paste and then crumple them up and knead them into a ball. In this way the paper absorbs the paste and makes it supple. Then carefully unfold the pieces again, possibly paint them once more with another layer of paste, tear them into small irregular pieces and start to cover your plasticine model with them (see figs. 105 to 107). The pieces of paper should overlap so that the first complete coat consists of about three paper layers. With this first layer as well as with the following ones it is very important to make sure that there are no air or paste bubbles between plasticine and paper, or between one layer of paper and the next. You should use smaller or larger pieces of paper according to the curvature of the model. You can smooth the surface with a bone paper-knife or your fingernail. If you find it hard to see the edges of the small pieces of paper on the model it means you have made a good job of it, and that the paper has been properly soaked and glued together. It also means that you can expect a smooth replica of your plasticine model. If, however, you have overlooked paste-bubbles and if you have not made sure that each piece of paper is properly glued, the durability of the head may be affected. If you use paper that is too wet, the final surface will become wrinkled and ugly. It is a good idea to use paper of a different colour for each layer applied. In this way you will be able to distinguish between the different layers and at the same time maintain an even thickness. The number of layers you will need will depend of course on the thickness of the paper used. Between 4 and 7 layers are usually sufficient, resulting in a gauge of about 1.5 mm when dried and finished.

Experienced puppet makers need about 2 or 3 hours for modelling a head in plasticine and about 4 hours for covering the model. In a well heated room the paper mould takes about 24 hours to dry, though it is always better to give it an extra day if possible.

When the paper mould is dry you must cut it in half and remove the plasticine. Usually the best place to cut it is 1 cm in front of the ear, or directly behind it (see fig. 106). Pierce the dry paper mould with a sharp, thin, pointed knife along the line you have decided to cut. Pierce hole after hole and do not try to cut by using a sawing movement. If you do, the edges will be damaged and you will have difficulty in joining the halves together again. Once you have cut the layer of paper, you have to cut carefully through the plasticine till the two halves separate. Always be careful not to damage the edges of the paper.

The next task is to remove the plasticine from both halves. A blunt table knife or a round spatula is recommended for this purpose. The empty insides have to be cleaned thoroughly with a rag. Plasticine contains oil, and this might in time penetrate the pasted paper layers, if it remains too long in contact with it.

Parts of the face that are specially vulnerable such as the nose or ears, should now be re-inforced from the inside. To do this it is sufficient to push paper balls kneaded in paste into these protruding parts and cover them securely with paper from the inside. Make sure that the re-inforcements are properly held to the parts they are supposed to strengthen or they may shrink when drying becoming detached and rattling about inside the head.

You may find that the re-inforcements have, in drying, created so much tension as to distort the halves of the paper mould so that they no longer fit together. Avoid this possibility by gluing the two halves together immediately after the re-inforcing process and before they have a chance to warp (fig. 107).

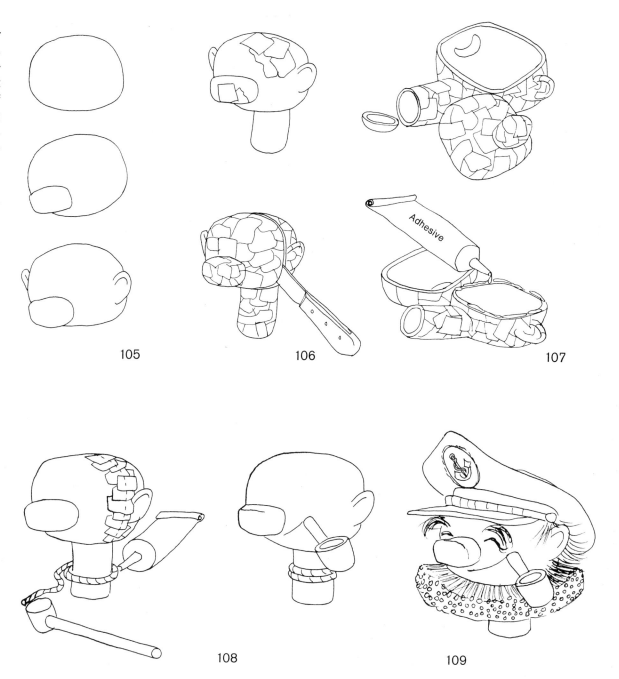

105

106

107

108

109

31

Bear in mind that if you wish to build into the head mechanical devices for manipulation (as described in Chapter VII), then this should be done before adding the re-inforcements, as you have to glue the two halves together immediately after re-inforcing them for the reasons given above. When gluing the two parts together use Uhu or Bostik and cover the seam with paper until it is invisible (fig. 108). In spite of all your efforts you might find the surface wrinkled in places. Do not despair, sand those parts down, or fill the recesses with plastic wood or putty and cover them again with paper and the wrinkles will disappear.

Glue a piece of cord round the neck as shown in fig. 108, thus forming a ridge which will make it easier to attach the glove puppet costume. Ideally the 'glove' of the costume should cover the puppeteer's arm up to about an inch above the elbow. If you enlarge fig. 110, it can be used as a pattern.

Modelling with sacking or cloth and glue:

Again the model is made of plasticine, and the same procedure of work applies as before (see figs. 111 and 112). Of course the model need not be made of plasticine; polystyrene, for instance is a very useful alternative and so is cardboard tubing (for special shapes) and wire netting and hessian.
Polystyrene is easily and quickly carved with a sharp knife and finished off with a rasp, file and sandpaper. As it has almost no weight it is often much more convenient to leave the model inside its shell without troubling to remove it. If you wish to cut

110

holes into the polystyrene for building in mechanical devices, use for preference a hot wire or blade, and if you want to remove the entire polystyrene model, hang the model and shell close above an open bottle of Acetone and put a paper bag over them. After a while you will find that all the polystyrene has gone and only the shell is left. Quicker results can be obtained by sprinkling some Acetone direct into the polystyrene. The precaution of the paper bag is necessary because the Acetone fumes have to be kept concentrated, and also because they are dangerous. When working with chemicals always be careful to safeguard yourself against accidents.

If you do not have access to large polystyrene blocks you can always build up to the required size by gluing pieces together with polystyrene glue (available from home decorating shops). Ordinary spirit-based glue such as Uhu or Bostik dissolves polystyrene straight away.

Hessian re-inforced with wire netting is used frequently in theatres as a supporting material for scenery and as a base for paper covering.

Cardboard tubes are especially good for three-dimensional trees and pillars. Sacking that has been thoroughly soaked in Scotch glue and draped over them makes them lose their geometrical straightness. Sacking used in this way gives the tubes irregularity and texture.

Whatever material you decide to use for covering your model, the procedure of work is always the same.

1. When making a model from plasticine or clay it is best to work on a glass, lino, or metal surface. On such a surface you can roll plasticine 'sausages', build them up to the desired shape by coiling them, pressing them together, filling in the grooves and generally smoothing the surface of the model (111).

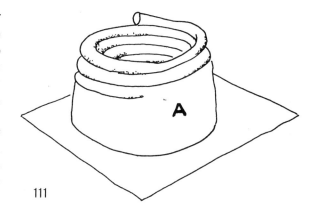

111

2. In order to strengthen the resistance of the finished plasticine model (112 A), protect it by covering it with one layer of paper and paste (112 B). This is not necessary if you use polystyrene, hessian re-inforced with wire netting, or cardboard tubing as a base.

3. On top of the part shown at B in fig. 112 — or straight on to the polystyrene as the case may be — you glue your pieces of sacking (112 C). (Sacking, hessian, pieces of cloth from old shirts, in fact any kind of cloth will do. Jersey cloth is particularly useful as it stretches and adapts to the shape of the model).

4. If for visual or practical reasons you need a smooth surface, put another layer of paper on top of the sacking (112 D). Or you can use plastic wood well sanded down.

Scotch glue, in the form of pearl glue or glue size is really best for the job, glue slabs are also good, but in preparation they take much longer to soak.

A brush, a sharp pair of scissors, a proper surface on which to paint your sacking, a cooker and a gluepot complete your working outfit.

As sacking and cloth have a rougher texture than paper, they are rarely suitable for delicate, small puppet heads.

Fill the upper container of the glue pot up to

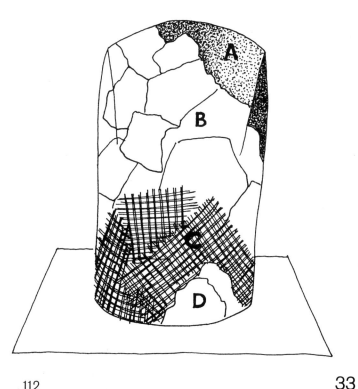

112

two-thirds full with pearl glue, then stir in cold water up to the brim and stir again a few minutes later in order to avoid the formation of lumps. Let the glue soak for at least one hour before heating it in the pot's water container. Never let the glue itself boil or it will lose its strength. By adding a 10 % proportion of alum to the glue its water-attracting quality is diminished and even when stored in a damp atmosphere your puppet heads will not get mouldy.

While the glue is being heated, cut your pieces of sacking. If a shape is as simple as the one in fig. 112, it is sufficient to have one big piece for the front and one for the back for each layer. You should use two or three layers of sacking depending on the purpose of the finished object, more of course if you use thinner material. As when working with paper, you have to avoid bubbles and wrinkles. The sacking must also overlap, but not each layer at the same place. Parts that are expected to stand up to particular strain should be strengthened straight away.

It is the glue, once set, that provides the stability and strength; the cloth and sacking act only as a supporting medium. Therefore it is necessary to saturate the material with glue by applying it generously on both sides and by giving the model itself a coat of glue before placing the saturated pieces of cloth on it.

Larger pieces of material will not fit round shapes of the model without wrinkling. Where wrinkles do occur, press any excess glue-soaked material together and remove by cutting off very close to the model. You

then have to push the two adjoining edges together and make sure that your second layer will cover this weak area properly.

The final shell should be between 1 and 3 mm thick, according to the wear and tear it is likely to encounter. If you leave the polystyrene model inside, one layer of sacking is usually sufficient.

After the glue has dried the surface is rough and almost spiky, so be careful to work on it with file and sandpaper until it is smooth. This usually is all that has be done when covering a model with sacking or cloth. Sometimes, however, a very smooth surface is wanted, and in such cases you should cover the sacking yet again with a layer of paper (112 D), but paper that is soaked in paste does not stick too easily to a surface of dried Scotch glue, and therefore you have to press and rub the pieces of paper on to the glue sacking to make them stick. If you should get an air bubble, cut it open, tear away all the paper near to it which is not firmly stuck, and then cover that particular area once again with pasted paper.

Another way to even out the rough surface of the sacking is by applying plastic wood or Polyfilla and sanding it down with fine sandpaper when dry. According to my experience, plastic wood is the most suitable of the two for this purpose.

If, for technical reasons, you have to cut holes into the dry paper or sacking shell with a knife, do so before removing the plasticine from within. If this is done the shell has some support from within and is less likely to collapse under the pressure of the knife. Also there is less likelihood that the

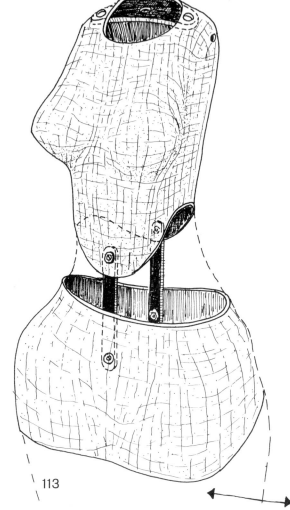

113

edges formed will be split or torn. The more holes you have, the easier it is to remove the plasticine. It is possible of course to cut the necessary holes after the removal of the plasticine with an electric key-hole saw, if you have one.

With bolts, nuts and large washers you can fix all sorts of handles and gadgets to the shells as you make them (see fig. 113).

34

CHAPTER IV

The Development of the Rod Puppet

Up to 1945 rod puppets were to be found only in the 'Hanneschen-Theater' in Cologne, the 'Aachener Schangche' and the former 'Stockpuppentheater der Elf Scharfrichter' in Munich. Elsewhere in Germany only two kinds of puppets were in use and these were the technically simple glove puppet worked from below, and the relatively complicated marionette or string puppet which, controlled from above, is operated against the force of gravity.

Of the two, the glove puppet is easier and cheaper to make and, what is more, the staging of a glove puppet show is a simpler undertaking than is the presentation of a string puppet performance.

A good glove puppet performer can do a show on his own as he can work two puppets at a time and can easily change from one character to the next. Moreover, as far as staging is concerned he needs nothing but a screen or booth in front of him. It is very different with a string puppet performance. Firstly a string puppeteer can only manipulate one puppet at a time, which means that more than one operator is needed to perform a play. Secondly, as string puppets are worked from above, a string puppet show demands a comparatively elaborate stage with a bridge structure from which the puppeteers can work. These facts have to be considered carefully when it comes to the choice of a puppet medium.

After 1945 the rod puppet emerged from comparative obscurity to have world-wide influence on the development of puppetry. Russian puppeteers were inspired by Asian puppets, especially the Javanese rod puppet known as Wayang Golek (see figs. 117 and 118) and the Japanese Bunraku Theatre (see figs. 145-153). Rod puppets became known and popular in Europe and the British Isles mainly through the Moscow Central Puppet Theatre directed by Serge Obratsov. The string puppet, which has always been regarded as of higher artistic calibre than the glove puppet has now found its rival in the rod puppet which has proved successful and is very much the fashion today; so much so that no puppeteer can afford to ignore it. But fashion and artistic standards are completely different things and we should not confuse them. As mentioned before the string puppet is at the mercy of the forces of gravity. It is a pendulum with moveable limbs. It can have legs and, worked from above, it can walk or fly through the air.

The puppeteer works at a distance from the puppet and his personal vitality reaches it very incompletely via the strings. Through the physical laws which the puppet obeys, quick powerful movements are not within its possibilities. But by its lightness, grace and ability to float through the air, those disadvantages are easily outweighed in the hands of a clever puppeteer. The technical skill that is required for the manipulation of the string puppet and the lack of personal contact between puppet and operator make many puppeteers today abandon the lyrical and graceful string puppet and turn to the more direct and immediate glove and rod puppets. But to choose a particular puppet medium is not only a matter of choosing a technique, it is also to a certain degree a choice of artistic intention. The designer and the director of a puppet show should adopt whichever technique has the greatest expressive potential for the particular play in question. Similarly every prospective puppeteer should ask himself which medium — glove, rod, or string — suits his temperament best.

But let us now discuss the different stages of development from the simple glove puppet to the complex rod puppet.

The most agile and lively hand puppet is the one which is fitted to the proportions of the hand of the operator (see figs. 114 and 115). The operator's index finger is inside the puppet's neck and works its head. The depth to which the index finger penetrates the head depends on the weight of the head; the heavier the head, the deeper it should go. The advantage of a light head is that it can be supported on the tip of the index finger. This allows a maximum range of movement for the finger and consequently maximum agility of the head. Glove puppet arms and hands are operated by thumb and middle finger, or by thumb and little finger. I think the most comfortable and practical way is to use thumb and middle finger as it makes the handling of props easy and definite. This is why most professional puppeteers use this method for aggressive figures like Punch, Policeman, Robber or Devil. As seen

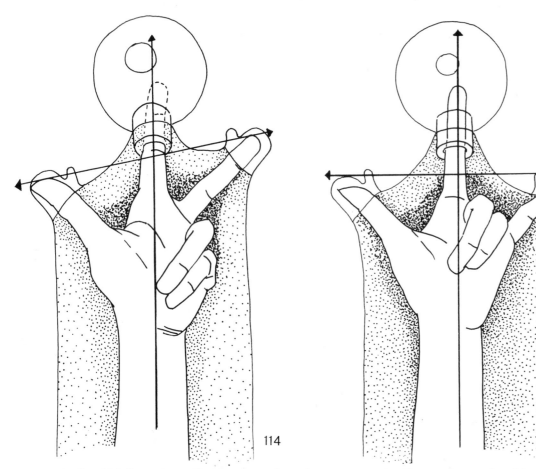

114

115

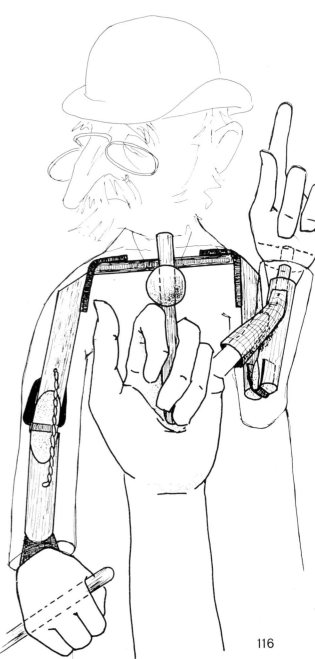

116

in fig. 114 there is a disadvantage to using thumb and middle finger in as far as this method leads to an asymmetrical position of the puppet arms. Therefore, when it comes to more dignified or beautiful members of the ensemble, the puppeteer tends to use thumb and little finger, although the little finger is less capable than the middle finger, as it makes for a straighter appearance of the puppet.

The width of the costume is determined by the span of the operator's hand. As with rod puppets, the costume should almost reach the puppeteer's elbow. The heads of these glove puppets should not be much larger than 10 or 14 cm. If they are too large they will look abnormal or even grotesque, though this can be counteracted if the puppet arms are lengthened at the same time. Because of the noise they make and their clumsiness in handling props, I do not recommend wooden puppet hands on cardboard-tube arms. Glove puppet hands made like mittens, using materials such as felt or cloth are much better to my mind. With this type the puppeteer pushes his fingers right into the puppet hands and can thus handle props with ease. The wrist of the puppeteer symbolizes the puppet's posterior. In special cases (as with Punch) the second hand of the operator has to help with the legs that dangle from the puppet's hips as in fig. 209. If the size of the hall you are to work in or the number of the audience you are to perform to necessitates the use of larger puppet heads, then the technique of arm manipulation as illustrated in fig. 116 is suitable. That is, of course, if you do not want to switch to rod puppets altogether.

The puppet shown in this drawing (116) represents an intermediate stage between glove and rod puppet. But to work it you need both hands and you cannot operate two puppets at a time, so once you have tried this method, you will probably want to move on to the rod puppet proper.

A simple example of a rod puppet is shown in figs. 117 and 118 illustrating a rod puppet from Java. The head movement of this puppet is somewhat restricted.

As a puppet's expression depends usually on bodily rather than facial movement, the wish to increase the rod puppet's possibility of movement has often led to technically complex figures. If done for specific characterisation the effect sometimes justifies the technical complexity, but for most puppets a simple construction is sufficient, and has the advantage of being able to be mass-produced. Time and again experience has shown that the simpler the mechanics the more convincing the movement of a puppet.

117

118

37

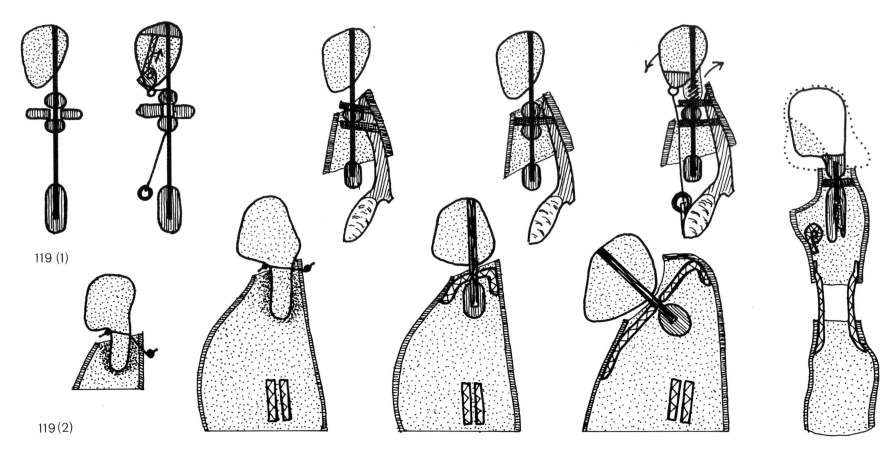

119 (1)

119 (2)

After having dealt at some length with theoretical considerations, we must now move on to the practical problems involved in planning and constructing a rod puppet. In figs. 119 (1), 119 (2), and 119 (3) we have the most important basic mechanisms in use today. Some of the drawings here are slightly simplified, others illustrate the mechanism fully.

Looking closely at them you will find that in some respects they are similar. Apart from those shown in 119 (2) they each have a combination of rod and handle by which an operator can carry them. The Javanese call this combination of rod and handle a 'gapit'. We have no word for it in any European language so I suggest that 'gapit' is adopted for common usage. The puppet-historian may interpret this as homage to the great Javanese rod puppet tradition. Gapits can also be built into the figures of 119 (2). The 'pistol grip' is a very popular and practical shape for a gapit, as it is well fitted to the hand, and as it leaves fingers free to press the levers or pull strings which operate the head.

The materials necessary for the construction of the puppets described are:

1. Hardwood dowel 10 to 14 mm in diameter.
2. Plywood of different thicknesses.
3. Wooden balls of different sizes (all these are available in 'do-it-yourself' shops or timber merchants).
4. Nylon string and lead weights (available in shops selling fishing equipment).
5. Wire of different thicknesses, screws, screw-eyes and washers.
6. Foam rubber.

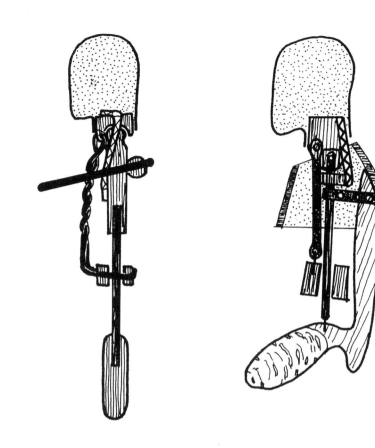

119 (3)

7. Cork plates for the handles (fishing equipment again).

8. Rubber from motor car inner tubes 3—6 mm thick (usually obtainable second-hand for nothing).

9. All the materials listed earlier for covering a plasticine model with glue and paper or hessian, (see Chapter III).

The illustrations under 119 (2) show a number of constructions without the combined handle and rod, and worked by a method which I have evolved myself. I was inspired by one of Rolf Trexler's puppets represented by the first figure in 119 (2).

These puppets are well covered with sacking and Scotch glue. In the lower part of their bodies and underneath the neck holes, stretched rubber strips are fastened to wooden re-inforcements with bolts and washers. The puppeteer slips his arm through the two lower strips of one of these puppets and as long as the tension of the rubber is properly calculated, the puppet will sit firmly on the arm held by the increase in circumference of the arm towards the elbow. This leaves the puppeteer's hand completely free for manipulating the head through the neck, or for handling the control rod. With his free hand he can also control a mobile puppet mouth or pair of eyes. No more explanation will be needed, I think, as the drawings are quite explicit.

I have throughout given, where possible, the names of the people whose ideas I have drawn upon. Refer also to the bibliography at the end of this book for further sources of information.

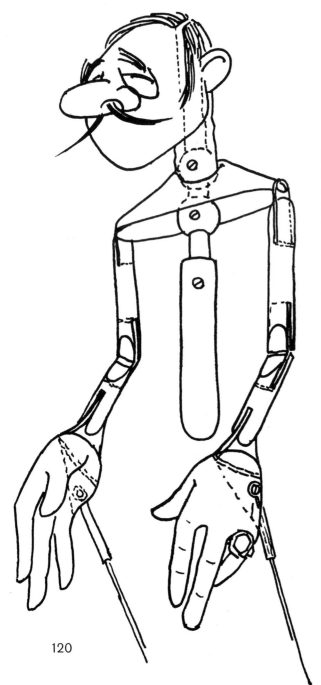

120

In fig. 120 we have a simple and popular construction for a rod puppet. It moves well, has pleasing proportions, can be mass-produced and yet the design still allows for life-like movement. From the manipulation rod the neckpiece goes right up to the skull of the puppet and is fitted to it at the top and at the back of the neck with 3 x 25 mm wood screws. It is advisable to use large washers between the screw's head and the skull in order to avoid any tearing. It is also a good idea to use screws rather than glue when fixing the neckpiece or the wooden ball to the handle as this makes it easier to dismantle the mechanism should this be necessary. If the dowel stick looks too thin as a neck, fasten a loose tube of jersey cloth to the back of the head and around the upper neck ball. As with the glove puppet it is the puppeteer's wrist that indicates the puppet's posterior. The arm joints are made of 1—2 mm thick leather, the best material for this purpose. This simple form of rod puppet is ideal for amateur performances in schools and for all those puppets which are not expected to perform any unusual tasks or move in any unusual way. The puppets shown in 101 to 104 are constructed according to the same principles.

The character in 121 is constructed in this way, except for the movable jaw. I designed this puppet for a production of 'Aladdin's Lamp'. During the early part of the performance its jaw did not move as it talked, and the audience was not aware of the fact that the jaw could move until towards the end of the play when the puppet became the victim of his own intrigue and lost his power of speech — a punishment which he had planned for somebody else. As soon as he could no longer speak his jaw started to move but no sound came from his mouth. This very effectively demonstrated his muteness.

As illustrated in fig. 121 a rubber band running between two screw eyes keeps the mouth shut. A nylon string, with a ring at the lower end, is fastened to the jaw to pull it open. In order to be able to anchor the lower screw-eye securely, the jaw should be made either entirely out of wood or be at least reinforced with wood.

The mechanism shown in figs. 122 and 123 is self-explanatory. With it you can bend the head from side to side or wobble it without interfering with its actual turning.

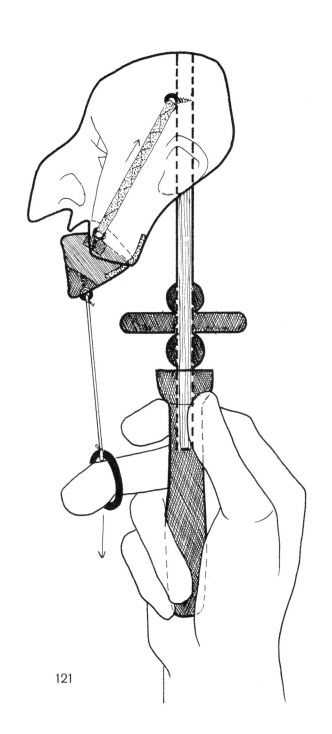

121

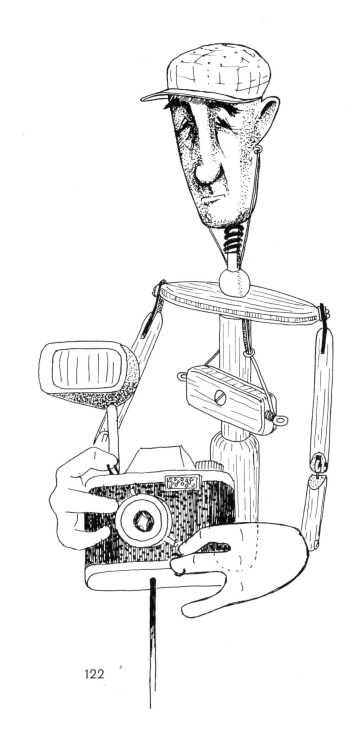

122

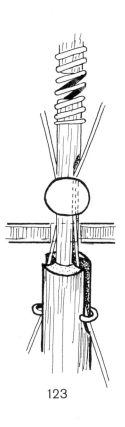

123

The trumpeter in fig. 124 is built according to the same principle. An accurately measured length of string brings the mouthpiece to the puppet's lips, and is held there by the ring at its lower end being looped over a screw-eye on the handle. The hands are loosely fastened to the trumpet with nylon string. If the manipulation rod fixed to the trumpet is cleverly operated, trumpet and hands can be made to move with the rhythm of the music. The construction shown in fig. 126 is rather more complicated. The head and shoulderpiece are made from paper or sacking and Scotch glue. Inside the back a piece of wood holds two screw-eyes which function as bearings for the ball joint. This joint is part of the neckpiece which is stuck into the pistol grip.

The eyes can open and close. They are mounted on and fixed to a common spindle. A rubber band running between two screw-eyes — one fixed to the inside of the nose the other to the eyeball — keeps the eyes open. The eyes can be made to close by pulling the nylon string which is fastened to the eyeball and runs through screw-eyes down the neck rod. The ring at the end of the nylon string can be connected to the handle with a rubber band, which makes it easier to find at any time during a performance.

The operator's thumb is placed inside a wire loop which is connected to the movable lower jaw. The angle of this wire depends on the position of the mouth and on the direction in which it is supposed to move. In special cases it might become necessary to introduce a hinge of some sort at the point where the wire is fixed to the jaw.

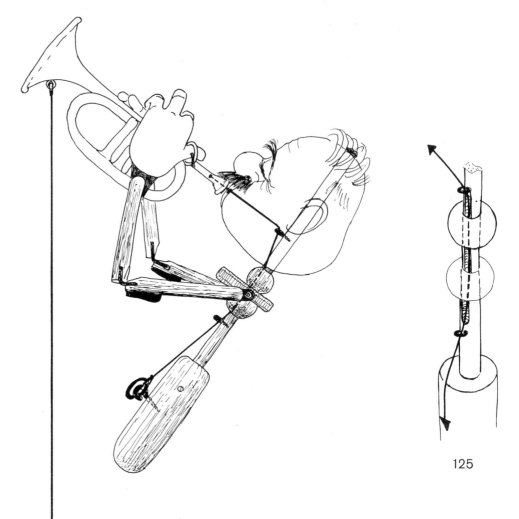

124

125

The construction of the village school teacher in figs. 127 and 128 is strong, simple and effective. 128 A illustrates the rubber band that keeps the two dowel ends together when the upper piece is not pulled over at an angle by the string. Leo von Uttenrodt made this puppet for a play called 'The Stolen Moon'. He has also devised and helped with a number of constructions shown

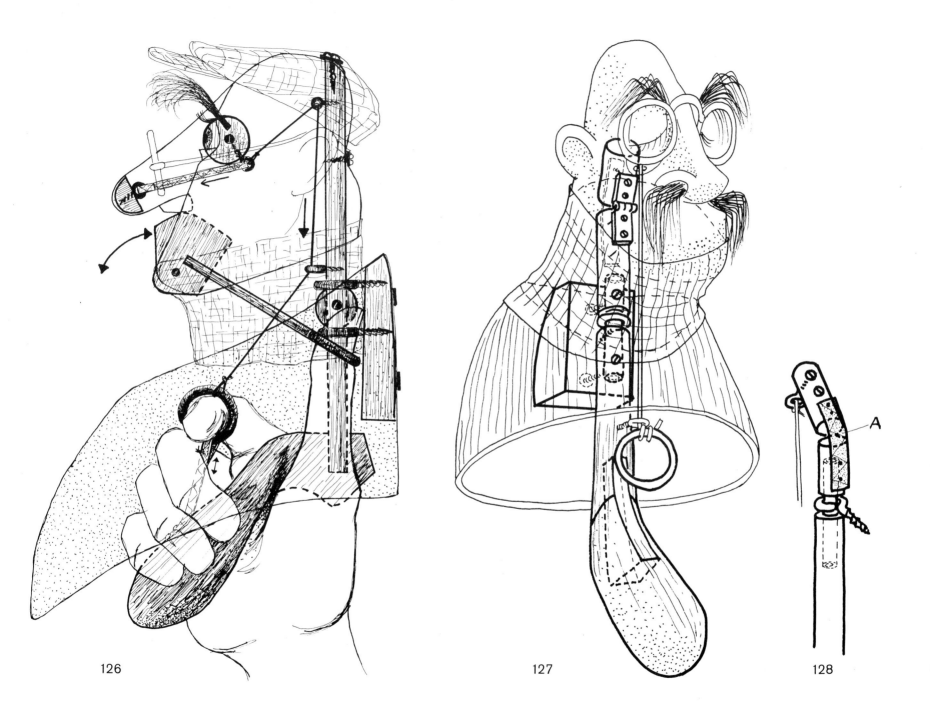

126

127

128

A

129

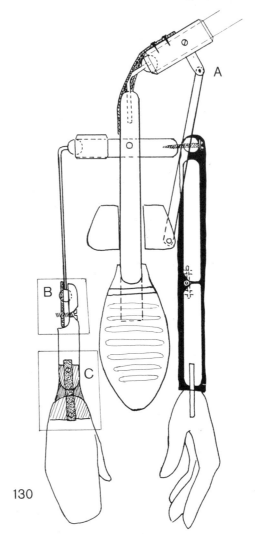

130

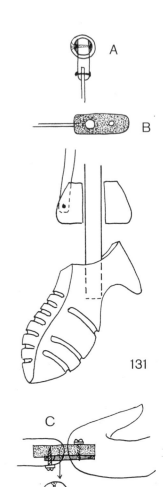

131

here. In the puppet museum in Munich I discovered Fritz Herbert Bross's 'Reading Grandmother' from Stuttgart, figs. 129 to 131. The arm supporting the newspaper has no manipulating rod as it is held in a fixed position by stiff ball-bearing joints. These ball-bearing joints were made by Bross himself in the following manner: detail B shows a metal ball and a brass plate with two holes.

The ball is fitted to the wooden armpiece and pressed against it by the plate which is screwed to the arm with a certain amount of tension. The dotted area on detail C is a brass rod fitted loosely into holes drilled into the hand and lower arm. A leather strip connecting hand and arm keeps them from slipping apart and restricts the amount of turning movement on the loosely fitting

44

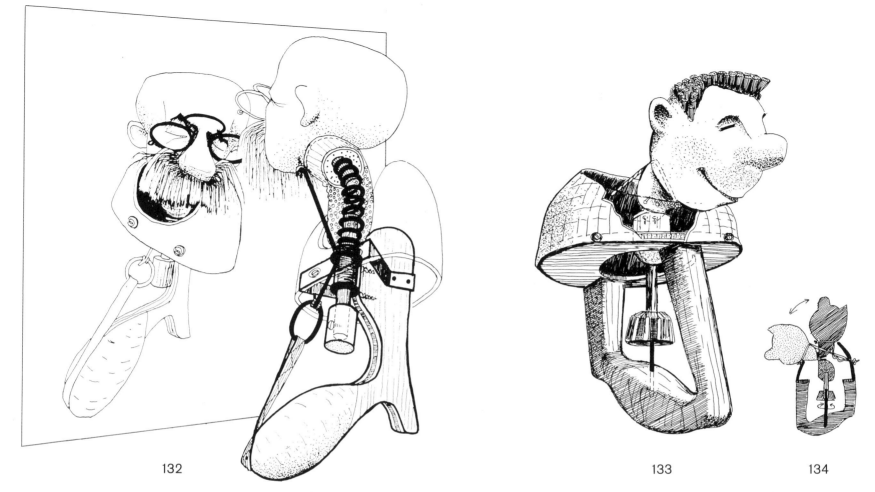

132   133   134

brass rod. This construction is rather complicated but the mechanical subtleties are definitely justified by the resulting effective movements, and a knowledge of them may come in very useful in dealing with special cases.

Another time-consuming, but very well functioning construction is 'Professor Karpenko' in fig. 132 (also from 'The Stolen Moon'), a puppet which Leo von Uttenrodt and I made together. The neck-spring is surrounded by foam rubber which supports it and gives it the right thickness. For aesthetic and protective purposes the foam rubber is covered with jersey cloth.

'Professor Karpenko's' assistant (133 and 134) was expected to look up to the stars a great deal so I made the neck-opening very wide. By turning the head control very quickly, the head fell right on to the back edge of the neck hole, and the nose of the puppet pointed straight upwards. By turning the control less vigorously, the head just looked to the side. By tilting the whole body slightly forward, the neck fell back into its normal position. The mechanisms for 'Karpenko' and for his assistant were devised for their specific characters and the tasks they were expected to perform in the play. The rather unusual movements these puppets made took the audience by surprise and helped to liven up the play. Both puppets, by the way, can be seen in the puppet collection which is a part of the Münchener Stadtmuseum.

45

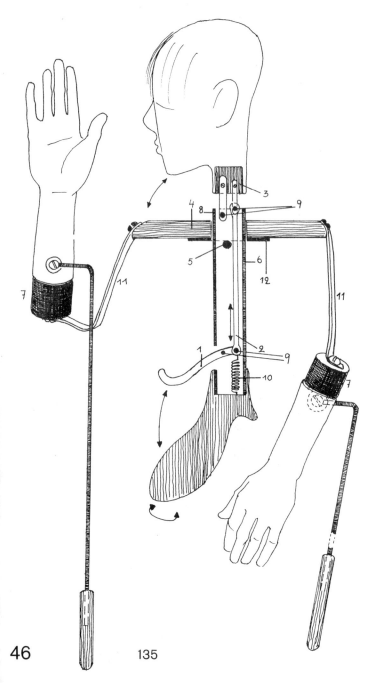

In fig. 135 another complicated yet excellent construction is shown. It was devised by Heinz Drescher, the director of the Weilheim puppet shows, who made the puppets for the German T.V. film 'Lili'. The arm manipulation deserves special attention. The manipulation rod, which is inside the costume and thus invisible to the audience, is fixed as close to the elbow as possible, just above the lead weight (7), which balances the weight of the lower arm. A strip of leather (11) connects elbow and shoulder (4) and stops the lower arm from swinging out of control. If the weight is properly balanced, this arrangement allows for absolutely exact arm manipulation. The degree of bend in the angle of the rod, the length of the short side of the angle and the length of the lower arm have to be determined individually for each puppet. If, for instance, you have a very short lower arm, the hand movement will look lively, but hardly anything of the arm is shown at all. If, however, the arm is long, the hand movement looks a bit stiff. With some skill and patient recognition of the possibilities you will soon find the right degree of compromise for your particular puppet. Here is an explanation of the numbers in 135:

① Lever with joints ⑨ for nodding the head.
② Rod with joint for nodding the head.
③ Piece of dowel for holding the head plus two small rods for the nodding mechanism.
④ Wooden shoulderpiece with a hole big enough for the aluminium tube ⑥ to turn freely.
⑤ Pin which holds both metal plate ⑫ and shoulderpiece in place.

⑧ Slot in the aluminium tube (not marked on the drawing) for the nodding action.
⑨ Joints.
⑩ Spring which pulls the head back into its normal position.
This mechanism is among the best I have ever come across.

When I visited Rolf Trexler's Rothenburger puppet theatre I learnt about the mechanism portrayed in figs. 136 and 137. It is extremely effective and at the same time very simple and practical needing only a piece of string fastened in the right places and a lengthened neck piece which serves as handle (gapit). For the operating of this type of puppet there are three different methods:

1. The head, separate and unfastened. is held in the operator's hand in the appropriate position relative to the body. This is a good method when a puppet must appear in several costumes in quick succession.
2. The same except that the head is secured as shown, with a piece of cord, to prevent it from slipping out accidentally.
3. Here a piece of rubber with a hole punched in the middle is put across the neck opening and fastened to the shoulders on either side as depicted in fig. 139. A wooden plug protruding from the head is pushed through the hole and fitted into a wooden ball of about 4 cm diameter underneath the rubber. All three methods have been proved to be excellent and the choice of their use is dependent on the particular requirements of the show.
I would like here to comment on how to costume this sort of puppet. As I personally

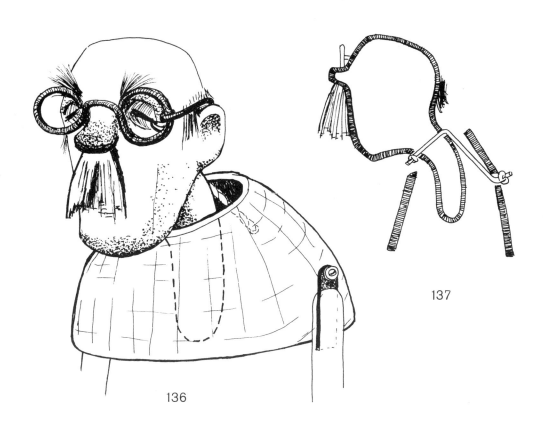

136

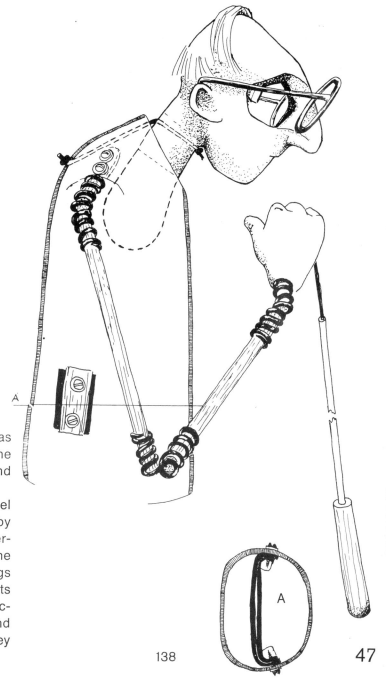

137

do not sew, I found myself in the difficult situation of having to instruct a costumier as to the size and proportion of the garment. As there was a good deal of confusion and misunderstanding, I decided to give my puppets proper bodies in order to be certain to get the correct size of costume.

Not only did this solve the problem of proportion, but it also saved a lot of time for the costumier who could now glue parts of the costume to the body instead of having to sew everything. But, of course, with this method the puppets became heavier. Therefore I fastened a strip of rubber to the body

138

136 A and slipped it over my lower arm (as described before) so as to distribute the weight and at the same time leave my hand free for manipulating the head.

The first puppets I saw with spiral steel spring joints were the marionettes made by the Werkakademie Kassel under the supervision of Professor Röttger. I found the swinging movement of their arms and legs so surprisingly lively that I tried spring joints on my own puppets. I found that they function well so long as they are correctly and firmly anchored. As soon as they slip they are useless.

47

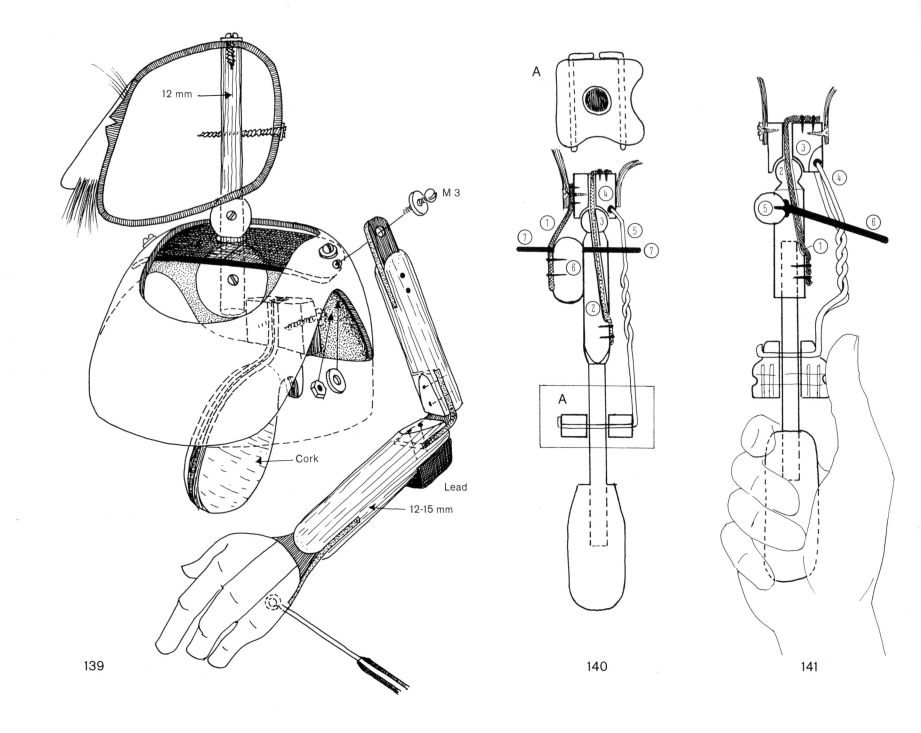

12 mm

M 3

Cork

Lead

12-15 mm

A

A

48   139   140   141

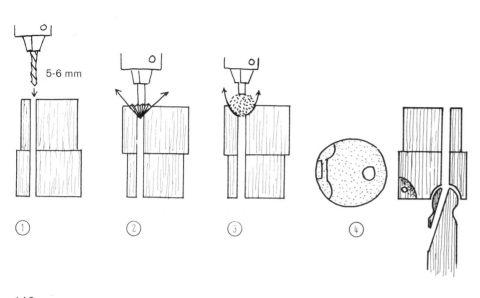

5-6 mm

① ② ③ ④ 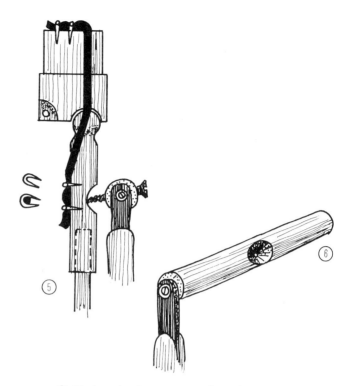 ⑤ ⑥

142

Although the two constructions in 140 and 141 look complicated, they are really quite easy to make and even quite easy to mass-produce. Figs. 142 ① to ⑥ explain the process. By turning the control of either 140 or 141 with the thumb, the puppet's head performs a circular nodding action. As the head is only slipped onto the neck rod and not fastened to it, it is easily exchangeable. These contrivances were first made by the Russians. They go a step further than Fedotow's constructions (described later[1]) and are an improvement on them. The controls shown in figs. 140 and 141, however, are

only successful if the individual parts are very accurately made and fitted. To start with you need hardwood dowelling of various diameters and a lathe on which to turn the ¾ of a wooden ball for the top of the control. Figs. 142 ① to ③ show how to make the bearing inside the neck piece. For the purpose of leverage the hole through the upper neck piece must be off-centre and towards the back of the neck ④. For the same reason the hole through the wooden ball has to be drilled at an angle. Here is an index to the parts shown in fig. 140:
① Rubber band for pulling the head back to its normal position.
② String for holding the neck piece ④ to the lower components.
③ Control with a wooden ball top.

⑤ Twisted wire connecting the control to the neck piece. This make the head nod and turn.
⑥ Wooden shoulder piece.
⑦ Wire which stops the costume from getting caught in the mechanism and also gives the puppet chest some bulk.
Construction 141 differs from 140 in one respect only, and that is that 141 ① unites the functions of 140 ① and ②. In other words, the strong piece of rubber does not only pull back the head into its normal position, but also holds the neckpiece together. The piece of rubber is fixed at both ends with wire staples, which should not pierce the rubber. If it does extreme tension may cause breakage at these points. Details are more clearly depicted in 142 ① to ⑥.

[1] Technik des Puppentheaters, Fedotow, VEB Friedr. Hofmeister, Leipzig.

These are the most important of the various mechanical devices applicable to ordinary rod puppets. Now let us discuss puppets which perform special movements and therefore need a special type of construction. For making such puppets the puppet maker needs a great deal of patience and constructive invention. I personally had much difficulty in working out the mechanics for 'Jenny' for a production of the 'Threepenny Opera'. I worked for about 100 hours on various attempts, before I arrived at the construction shown in figs. 143 and 144.

Jenny was supposed to wriggle her shoulders and bosom while keeping her head absolutely still. Then it had to be possible for her shoulders to be still while her head moved independently. And finally, she was expected to walk moving her hips in a seductive fashion.

As one arm was permanently fixed to the hip, the puppet needed only one arm rod. Shoulders and chest were operated by the puppeteer's thumb and the neck by alternate backward and forward movements of the middle and index finger. Straightening or bending these two fingers from their lowest joints makes the puppet neck stretch or relax, and it is for this purpose that both the wooden pieces are rounded off. A special wire loop is fastened onto the shoulders and supports the mechanism without danger of it getting jammed. By operating the upper part of the body as described and simultaneously turning and pushing the hip part, the illusion of a very sexy walk is created. In such a case the right arm hangs down and is not operated except for the indirect swing it gets from the movement of the shoulders.

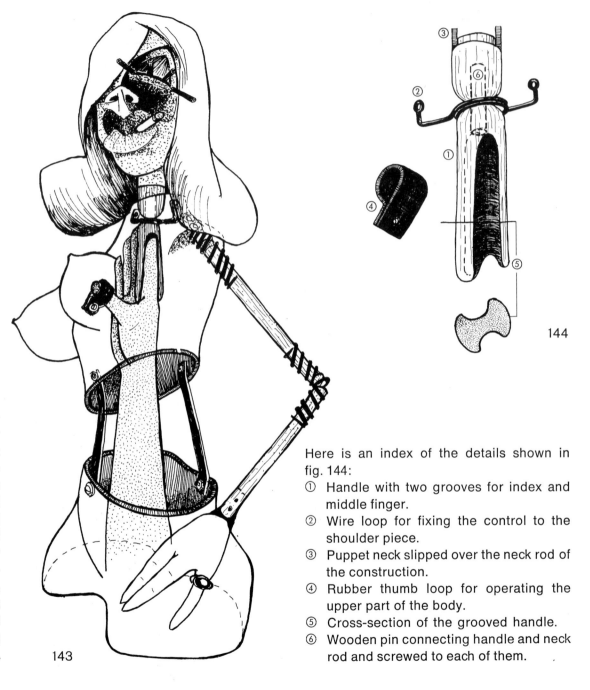

143

144

Here is an index of the details shown in fig. 144:

① Handle with two grooves for index and middle finger.
② Wire loop for fixing the control to the shoulder piece.
③ Puppet neck slipped over the neck rod of the construction.
④ Rubber thumb loop for operating the upper part of the body.
⑤ Cross-section of the grooved handle.
⑥ Wooden pin connecting handle and neck rod and screwed to each of them.

The Japanese Bunraku puppet, see figs. 145 to 153, is the most complete, the most complicated and probably the most sophisticated rod puppet in the world. Richard Teschner was the only puppet maker in Europe to achieve anything comparable. He was strongly influenced by Javanese and Chinese puppets as you can see from his work shown in a book entitled 'Richard Teschner und sein Figurenspiegel'[1].

From an old Japanese book, which the custodian of the puppet museum in Munich was kind enough to lend me, I have tried to find out how Bunraku puppets are built. And in spite of the fact that I could not read a single word of this book, and that the drawings were not very explicit, I think I have grasped the main principles of the technique pretty well. Fig. 145 shows how a Bunraku puppet is operated. Three puppeteers appear with it on the stage, while the speaker for the puppet reads the text at the side of the stage to the accompaniment of the Samisen orchestra. The three operators are of different professional status. With his left hand the first operator manipulates the head of the puppet through a hole in its back and with his right hand works the puppet's right arm. He wears a costly kimono and has no mask over his face. The second puppeteer in fig. 145 operates the left arm of the puppet which usually has a hand with movable fingers, and the third puppeteer operates the feet. Both second and third operators wear black gowns with hoods over their faces. These hoods have slits for the puppeteers to see through.

[1] Richard Teschner und sein Figurenspiegel, Dr. Franz Hadamowsky, Eduard Wancura Verlag, Wien/Stuttgart.

145   1   3   2

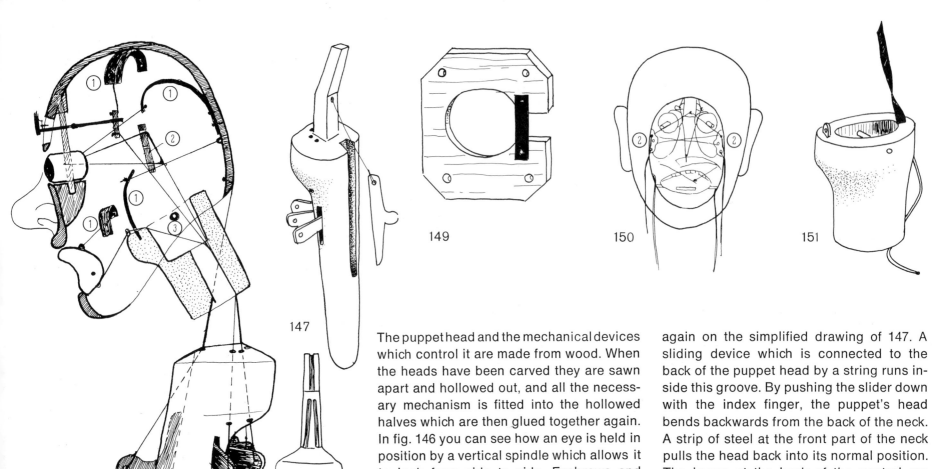

149

150

151

147

146

148

The puppet head and the mechanical devices which control it are made from wood. When the heads have been carved they are sawn apart and hollowed out, and all the necessary mechanism is fitted into the hollowed halves which are then glued together again. In fig. 146 you can see how an eye is held in position by a vertical spindle which allows it to look from side to side. Eyebrows and lower lip are also movable. All these parts are connected to the main control by strings and worked from there with the aid of a number of levers. Strips of steel function as springs 146 ① which pull the movable parts back into their normal positions again. The parts numbered ② in figs. 146 and 150 are two pieces of wood through which the controlling strings are led. The horizontal spindle or shaft ③ connects head and neck, allowing the head to nod. Down the front of the control runs a T-shaped groove, shown

again on the simplified drawing of 147. A sliding device which is connected to the back of the puppet head by a string runs inside this groove. By pushing the slider down with the index finger, the puppet's head bends backwards from the back of the neck. A strip of steel at the front part of the neck pulls the head back into its normal position. The levers at the back of the control are operated individually by the puppeteer's thumb. The neck piece rests loosely inside a hole in a piece of wood as shown in fig. 149 in such a way as to allow the neck to turn. This piece of wood is loosely attached to the wooden shoulder piece with four strings, see figs. 152 and 153. Fig. 153 shows the upper, 152 the lower side of the construction. Thus loosely held, the head is extremely mobile. Not only can the head nod and turn, but also sink into the shoulders and pop up again.

The body constists of a wooden hoop for hips and two lengths of padded cloth which are just flexible enough to enable the puppet to move naturally. Body and limbs are fastened to the shoulder piece with string (see holes for string in figs. 152 and 153). It takes a lot of practice to be able to operate such a puppet and that is why a Japanese puppeteer has to learn for 10 or 20 years before he is permitted to take the part of the first operator, i. e. the one who works the head and the right arm of the puppet.

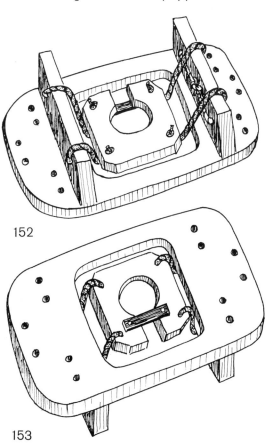

152

153

154

To round off this chapter on construction and technique for rod puppets, I should like to mention a few more special cases. They are all more or less successful, but can when amateurishly made, do more harm than good to the reputation of puppetry. They are generally very difficult to handle and, as said before, can only be regarded as fringe members of our ensemble.

In fig. 154, for instance, we have a belly-dancer. The long pole that turns her head and goes right through her entire body unfortunately makes her very stiff. If the head were somehow skilfully hung from the pole, the general effect of the puppet's movement might be improved, but the amount of work involved in doing this would probably be disproportionately great in comparison with the results obtained. Very ingenious, however, is the diagonal interconnection of chest and hips. If you rock the cross-bar at the lower end of the control, upper and lower part of the body move in opposing d'rections. Perhaps this device could be used more effectively with some other puppet.

53

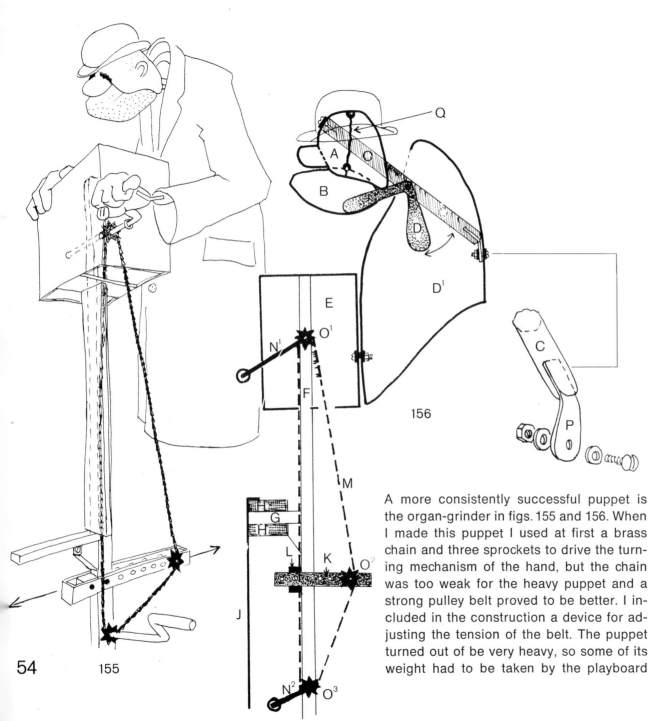

155

156

with the aid of a wooden wedge (G) held by the playboard (H).

The following letters stand for:

A   Upper part of the head.

B   Movable lower jaw.

C   Control rod.

D   Lever for the lower jaw.

D 1 Hollow body made with paper or hessian and Scotch glue.

E   Barrel organ box.

F   Main support for puppet and mechanism.

L, K Drilled movable plate for increasing the tension of the chain or belt.

N 1, N 2 Crank handles.

O 1, 2 and 3 Sprockets.

M   Chain

P   Leather joint connecting the body to the head control.

Q   Rubber band which pulls the lower jaw back into shut position.

The other arm of (D) extends into (B), but is not fixed there. The head can tilt forwards and backwards and sideways; its range of movement is dependent on the width of the opening made for the neck.

Figs. 157 and 158 depict the construction of a puppet representing a comical soprano. It was planned that she should open her mouth widely, open and close her eyes, breathe heavily and in addition her sagging cheeks should vibrate. Head and lower jaw were made in the form of a hollow shell of paper and glue (as described in Chapter III). Her shoulders and the padding for her hair were made of polystyrene and the mechanical parts of plywood, hinges and rubber bands. The gap between upper and

A more consistently successful puppet is the organ-grinder in figs. 155 and 156. When I made this puppet I used at first a brass chain and three sprockets to drive the turning mechanism of the hand, but the chain was too weak for the heavy puppet and a strong pulley belt proved to be better. I included in the construction a device for adjusting the tension of the belt. The puppet turned out of be very heavy, so some of its weight had to be taken by the playboard lower jaw was covered by two bags of jersey cloth (not shown in the drawing) which represented the sagging cheeks. Her hair was of white Angora wool with a slight purple tinge. The pistol grip of the control was of cork comfortably shaped. The mouth is opened by placing the index finger through the hole in the plywood and pulling it down. And the chest is operated with the third and little finger. The eyes are pulled open with the aid of a nylon string. The eye mechanism (not shown here) is the same as that in fig. 267. In order to make this puppet work well two puppeteers should operate it as shown in fig. 164.

Serge Obrazov, the famous Russian puppeteer and Director of the Central Puppet Theatre in Moscow, owns a puppet such as this and operates it by himself. To achieve this he fixes the costume and puppet head to a special cap which he places on his head for a performance. The costume masks his head and shoulders as demonstrated in fig. 159. As he supports the entire puppet on his head, both arms are left free for the manipulation of the puppet's arms, though in this particular case Obrazov uses his own hands for the hands of the puppet. During the puppet's song Obrasov's hands fiddle with her necklace and, through the necklace, eyes and mouth are controlled.

This kind of puppet is called, for obvious reasons, a head puppet. On fig. 159 a normal rod puppet control is mounted on a plastic helmet. As the puppeteer cannot see what he is doing, this way of operating is not highly recommended except in very special cases.

157

158

159

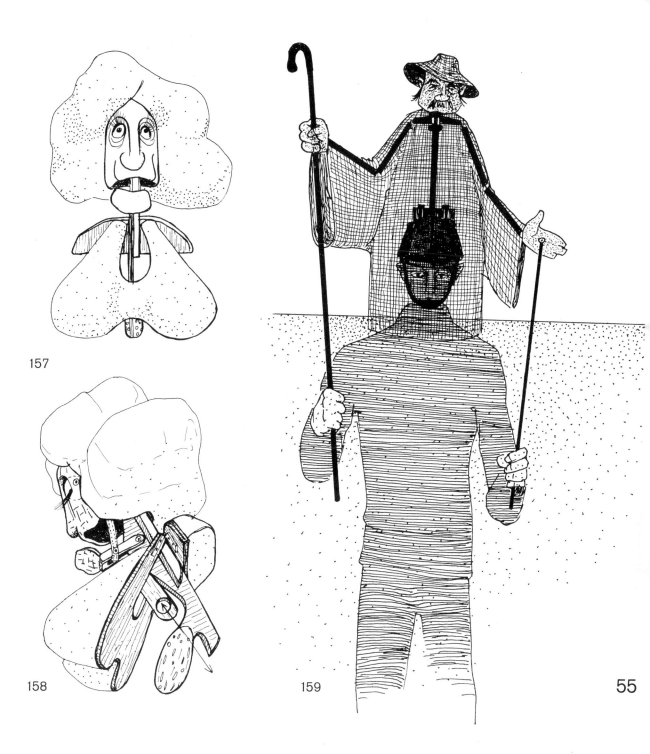

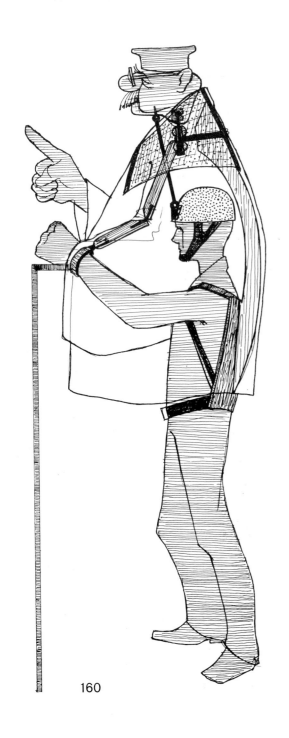

160

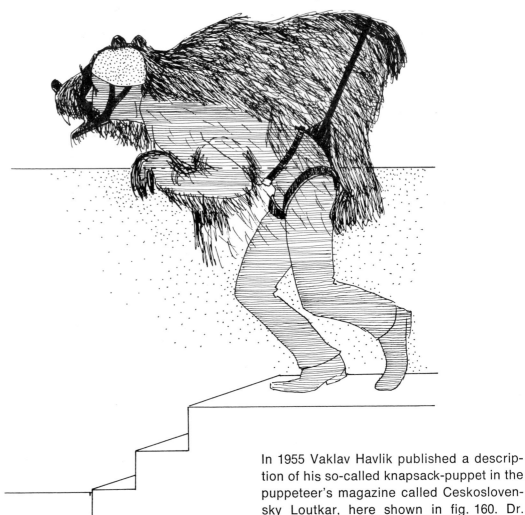

161

In 1955 Vaklav Havlik published a description of his so-called knapsack-puppet in the puppeteer's magazine called Ceskoslovensky Loutkar, here shown in fig. 160. Dr. Purschke published the article in Germany in 'Perlicko-Perlacko'. The part of a giant could be very effectively played by such a puppet as the head is nice and mobile. The bear in 161 is constructed according to the same idea. With a bit of skill the puppeteer's lower jaw can transmit mouth movements to the bear's jaw.

In fig. 162 you see depicted two street sweepers. In both cases the puppet's arms are manipulated through the broomsticks they hold, a very simple, ingenious and effective way of operating. The puppeteer on the right handles the broomstick directly, the one on the left uses a manipulation rod connected to the broomstick. The direct handling seems to me to allow for more accurate control.

Usually, large puppets are very heavy, and for this reason the puppets in the Cologne Haenneschen Theatre are supported from the ground on long telescopic poles. But puppets supported in this way obviously cannot move about much, and the method illustrated in fig. 162 for taking the excessive weight of a puppet is to be preferred. The operator wears a belt with a leather socket which holds a short bamboo pole which, in turn, supports the puppet.

I visited Rolf Trexler's puppet theatre in Rothenburg and found it most inspiring. I consider that a journey to see his work is well worthwhile. His snake charmer, for instance, I thought was a most fascinating puppet, with an excellent system of control. In fig. 163 I have tried to depict and analyse this puppet from memory. The snake charmer's pipe is worked very much in the same way as the trumpet mentioned previously.

162

57

163

When the character first came on stage, the audience could not see his legs but he sat sideways on the playboard, lifted one leg over it, turned and then lifted the other. Then he looked for some time at each foot alternately. He made a few remarks on their state of cleanliness and finally crossed his legs with the soles of his feet uppermost. After he had prepared himself in this manner, he started to play his pipe. The puppet has no knee joints. The legs are worked with the aid of a handle above each knee. These handles are made of strips of rubber. It was also through Rolf Trexler that I became acquainted with the so-called 'miming' puppet, an example of which is shown in fig. 164. To work it two manipulators

are needed. The head of a 'miming' puppet, or at least half of it, is made of flexible material, and there are several ways of making such a head:

1. The head, without the lower jaw, is modelled in plasticine and covered with paper and glue. Lower jaw, nose and the roof of the mouth are made of cloth and possibly stuffed with cottonwool. These parts are then glued or sewn to the rigid upper part of the face. The puppeteer puts his hand right through the neck and into the head of the puppet. He places his thumb into the lower jaw, his middle finger into the nose and his third and index fingers into the eye-sockets, (that is if these are made of cloth as well). By clever movement of the manipulator's hand and fingers the puppet can actually be made to pull faces.

2. The whole head is made of cloth and stuffed in parts.

3. The head is made of soft cast rubber. This technique with detailed descriptions of procedure is given in Chapter VI, see fig. 204. It is very important to have the opening of the neck wide enough for the puppeteer's hand to get through. In order to accommodate the hand of the operator the head of this kind of puppet has to be rather large, and so the puppet's hands must be large accordingly. For this reason a puppeteer can use his own hands without spoiling the proportions of the whole.

Some puppeteers, in doing this, show their hands without covering but this has always struck me, personally, as a breach of style of some sort and I prefer these human puppet hands to appear in gloves.

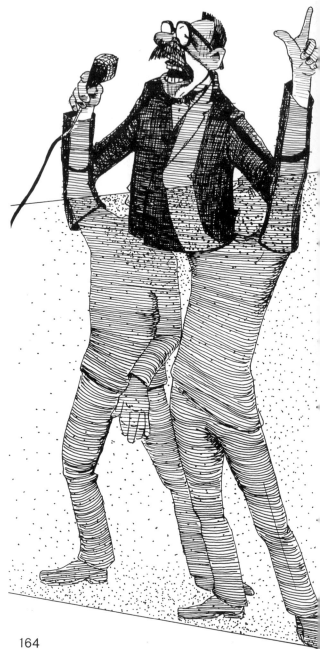

164

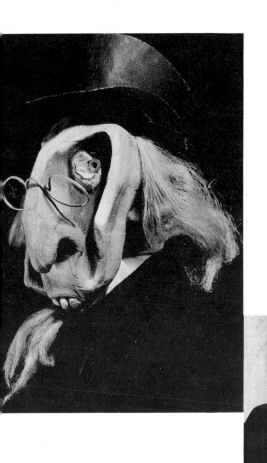

CHAPTER V

Proportions of Puppet Figures

The ordinary glove or rod puppet is between 30 and 50 cm high and, as a rule, has a fixed expression on its face. Puppet heads with mobile eyes, eyebrows, mouths or ears are the exceptions. Bearing these facts clearly in mind let us examine closely the characters shown in figs. 165 to 179 with regard to the relationship in size between their heads, bodies and limbs.

The human head measures about a seventh of the entire height of a person. A puppet, however, should have different proportions and it is generally accepted that it is most effective if its head is a quarter to a sixth of its visible height. In order to be able to gauge the correct proportions of a puppet, the glove and rod puppet designer should imagine that he is designing puppets with legs. The dotted areas in fig. 165 A, B, C, and D are not visible to the audience, the black line indicates the height of the playboard or screen behind which the puppeteer works. Although the part of the puppets below the playboard will be neither made nor seen, the designer should pretend he is making a marionette with legs so as to get the proportions right. '1' in figure 165 D indicates the entire height of the puppet. Three quarters of it are seen above the playboard. If we assume the visible height of this cook to be 40 cm, we would have to divide 40 by 3 to arrive at the measurement for his head, in this case 13.33 cm. As the cook's hat is

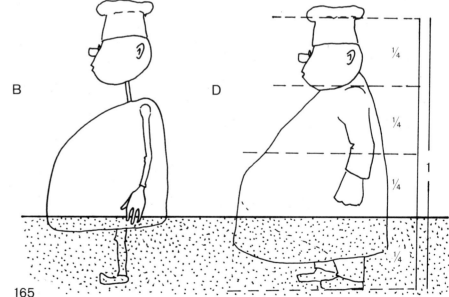

165

responsible for part of the height, the correct height of the head itself would be about
11 or 12 cm.

Now let us examine the puppet's arms. The
pendant arms of an upright puppet should
be fully visible to the audience. Quite apart
from aesthetic considerations, longer arms
would make manipulation difficult. In figs.
165 A and B a very common mistake is illustrated. Although both head and body are
fat, the general impression is not that of a
fat puppet. This is for two resaons: firstly
body and head have the wrong proportions
(the body is too small for the head), secondly, neck and limbs are far too thin in relation
to the rest of the puppet. The necks of fat
people are usually even thicker than their
heads. Figs. 165 C and D verify this state-
ment.

With slender characters, however, a thin
long neck is a very important and expressive
descriptive feature, see figs. 173 to 178. The
impression of the character's thinness is
emphasised by his stem-like neck and his
tall top hat. The head of the character
shown in fig. 175 is about a fifth of his whole
height. Assuming the visible height of this
puppet to be 50 cm, we should divide 50 by
4 to arrive at the measurement of the head.
This gives us 12.5 cm, not counting the top
hat.

Fig. 166 shows how you can design a fat
character from a spherical shape. It is advisable to make fat puppets by covering a
plasticine model with paper and glue (as
described in Chapter III) but thin puppets,
are best constructed as shown in figs. 120,
140 and 141.

166

167

168

169

170

171

172

The series of drawings 167 to 172 and 173 to 178 demonstrates how essential body and head movement are to the dramatic effect of a puppet.

167 Mr. X walks home with his nagging wife feeling crushed and depressed.
168 He escapes from the old dragon. He feels free and happy, and walks, whistling, towards the pleasures of an evening in a pub. 169 Something attracts his attention and he stops, saying to himself: 'Wait a minute. What's going on here?'
170 He calls out: 'Hey, you sir, keep your hands off that lady!'
171 'What's that you say? Its not my busi-ness? Just you wait a minute and I'll show you whether or not this is my business!'
172 'Oh dear, this is what happens if you interfere in other people's affairs.'
The expression of the face is always the same, it is the movements of the head and the body which give meaning to the action of the plot.

173 Mr. Y struts along briskly.

174 Suddenly he asks himself: 'What's this?'

175 'Am I mistaken?'

176 'No, I can hear it again quite distinctly!'

177 'Oh dear, I must run as quickly as I can.'

178 'Every man for himself!'

Good puppetry is movement, puppets who do nothing but recite words are boring. Throughout each scene it must be the movement that explains the story, the words should play a secondary role in the process of unravelling the plot. As puppet movement is so very important, we must devote some time in the following chapters to the exact technical requirements of good puppet movement.

63

179

of depression in contrast with that of his resolute, corsetted wife. With this couple the relative position of their heads is similarly telling.

I drew these characters intending to illustrate the different meaning of shapes. I had no idea of any scene or plot. Now that I see these figures in front of me I ask myself immediately what sort of relationship they have to each other and for what purpose they are meeting. It came to my mind that the three darkish characters might just have come from a funeral service and are on their way to join the heirs for a discussion on the division of property over a meal.

Many a novelist, I understand, starts his work by inventing his characters. He then thinks of their temperaments, their social background, and the situations in which one meets the other. Once the characters start to function, the plot seems to progress of its own accord as the action of one character provokes the reaction of another who, in turn is motivated by his social background, his education etc. Of course there may be some range of choice in the character's reactions and it is up to the author to choose that which best promotes the intention of his work. Once the author has created his characters, they become his partners and he must stop treating them arbitrarily. The same is true of the relationship between puppeteer and puppet. To the puppeteer who handles him, a puppet will suggest a particular voice and a manner of movement and these the puppeteer will be compelled to adopt.

If we look at the cook and Mr. Y in fig. 179, we realise that those two characters are similar in style and could belong to the same ensemble. Yet, on the other hand, they are so very different in shape that even from the back row of the theatre, a spectator could not confuse them. They are characterised so strongly by movement and body shape that even when their facial expression becomes invisible they unequivocally retain their identity.

Mr. and Mrs. X from 167 also fit the style of cook and Mr. Y. And although there are three fat people standing close together (cook, Mr. X, and Mrs. Y) there is no mistaking them for one another. Although Mr. X is fat, he is not as fat as the cook. The husband's drooping carriage gives him an air

CHAPTER VI

Puppet Arms and Puppet Legs

Puppet Arms:

The arms of rod puppets are manipulated with the aid of thin dowel sticks or with tensile steel rods. These can be outside the body of the puppet or within it. If they are outside, construction is comparatively easy and, in operation wide gestures can be made, but the fact that the rods are visible may be considered a disadvantage. The best inside manipulation method, to my mind, is shown in fig. 135.

Two other ways are shown in 181 and 182. Both of these are from Russian puppets again as described in Fedotow's book[1]. In both cases upper and lower arms are joined by means of a small flap hinge. Up and down the manipulating rod runs a thumb-operated sliding device. This device is connected to the lower arm by a string which runs over a short brass screw with an appropriate shank, or over a pin put across the slot of the upper arm just beneath the leather joint of the shoulder. In fig. 181 the hand is fastened to the lower arm with a leather joint giving it very limited movement. In 182 the hand is part of the lower arm with no separate movement at all, but here the relative angle of the lower arm to the hand

[1] Technik des Puppentheaters, A. Fedotow, German version Jutta Balk, Publ. Friedrich Hofmeister, Frankfurt.

differs from that shown in the previous drawing (181). A third alternative to this method of joining the hand to the lower arm whilst allowing a certain amount of independent hand movement can be seen by referring back to figs. 130 and 131 (c), (Fritz-Herbert Bross). There we also find two very interesting ball joints. The making of the left one will be discussed later. The right one consists of a wooden ball fastened by means of a screw to the shoulder-piece. The ball is sewn into the sleeve without being directly connected to the wooden arm-pieces.

But let us refer again to fig. 180. Here we see illustrated the most common rod or string puppet arm. Both upper and lower arm are made of hardwood dowelling measuring 10 to 20 mm in diameter. Although the weight increases with the thickness of the dowel, thicker arms are recommended as they are much more durable. Above the elbow a weight is fastened to the upper arm. This is necessary to counter-balance the hand. There is no way of determining how heavy it should be but by trying. The best weights to use are those obtainable in shops which sell fishing tackle, or strips of lead which can be wrapped around and nailed to the upper arm. If no weight is used there is a risk that the elbow will tip upwards as soon as the hand is turned in a certain direction. The heavier the hand the more likely it is that this will happen. In this respect, therefore, hands made of balsa wood have an advantage. Hands made from this light wood, however, are inclined to break easily, but they can be strengthened by soaking them in

varnish or, better still, covering them with glue and paper. All joints in this arm (fig. 180) are made with strips of leather which are inserted into slots and glued in place with cold glue. For additional strength and security two pins on either side of the joint are carefully nailed through wood and leather. It is important to put the pins in with great care as the wood tends to split at these points, therefore one should blunt the point of the nail by tapping it with a hammer whilst holding the head of the nail against a solid metal surface.

The way in which the rod is fastened to the hand or arm is determined by the movement it is supposed to perform. It can either be attached to the side of the hand as shown in fig. 180, or to the middle of the palm. A metal washer should be put between the hand itself and the wire loop of the rod and another between the wire loop and the head of the screw. This ensures smooth manipulation of the rod. The screw must be loose enough to allow the wire loop to move freely in one direction. If it is too loose, however, the loop will move in more than one plane and this will impair the manipulator's control over the movement.

The arm with the hinged joint in fig. 183 can perform one limited movement. The elbow cannot bend backwards as lower and upper arm touch each other when the hinge is open. The angle at which the two arm pieces are cut determines the rest position of the arm. If instead of being trimmed at right angles the ends are cut at an angle of 100 ° or 120 ° the rest position will be that of a slightly bent arm instead of a straight one.

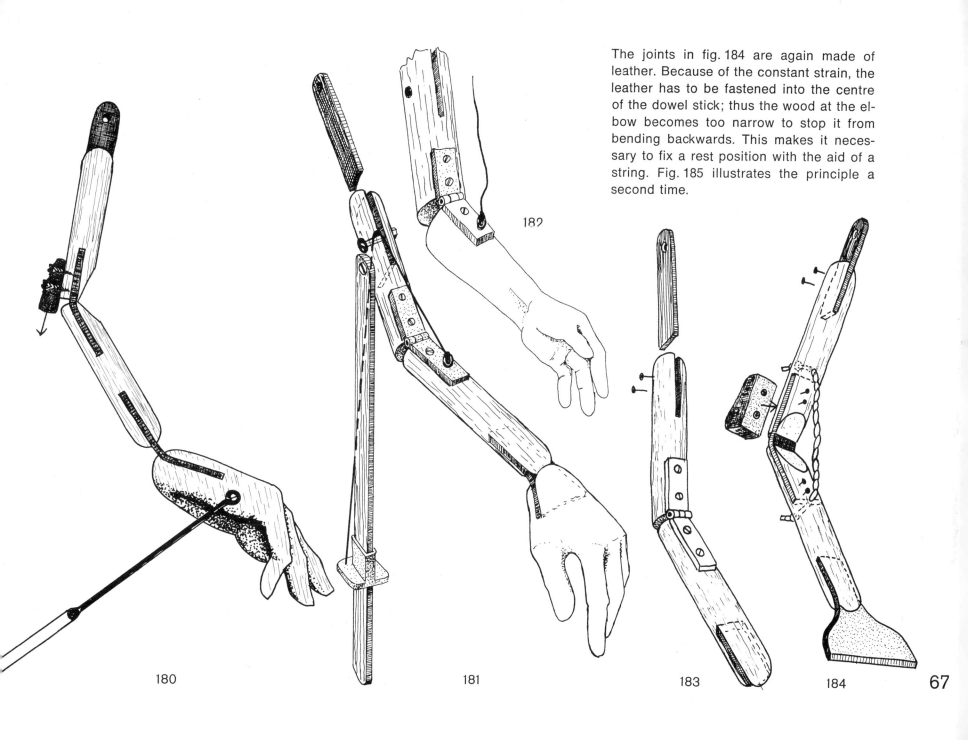

The joints in fig. 184 are again made of leather. Because of the constant strain, the leather has to be fastened into the centre of the dowel stick; thus the wood at the elbow becomes too narrow to stop it from bending backwards. This makes it necessary to fix a rest position with the aid of a string. Fig. 185 illustrates the principle a second time.

182

180

181

183

184

67

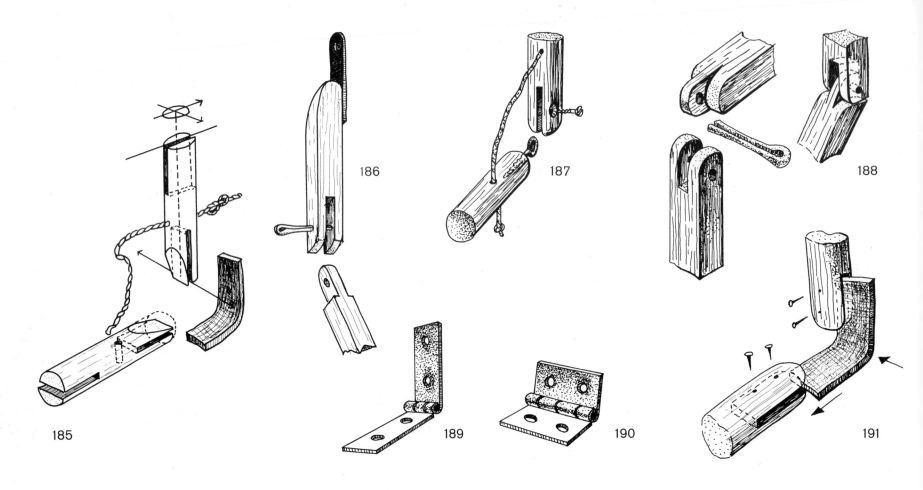

185

186

187

188

189

190

191

Very important also are the angles of the slots which take the leather strips in the arm pieces. Generally the shoulder slot is sawn at 90 degrees to the elbow-slot. However, there is no general rule for the angle of the hand-slot, it is different in each individual case depending on the required position of the hand.

Figs. 186-191 show further variations of hinge jointing. Most of these are quite easy

to make. When producing a number of puppets it is advisable to prepare a block of wood as shown in fig. 192. Once this device is made and properly fitted into the circular saw, the slots can be cut quickly and precisely with the same depth each time. It also helps to diminish the danger of cutting in one's fingers. The front elevation (A), the side elevation (B), and the perspective drawing, show how this block of wood is made. It is

obvious that the marks on top of the block help to find the required angles when cutting the slots.

Ball-joints also are not difficult to make (see figs. 193 and 194). First a hardwood dowel-stick or an iron rod of the same diameter as the ball has to be rounded off at one end. This dowelstick or rod is fitted into a brass or iron tube which is beaten with a chasing-hammer till the dowel cannot slip through.

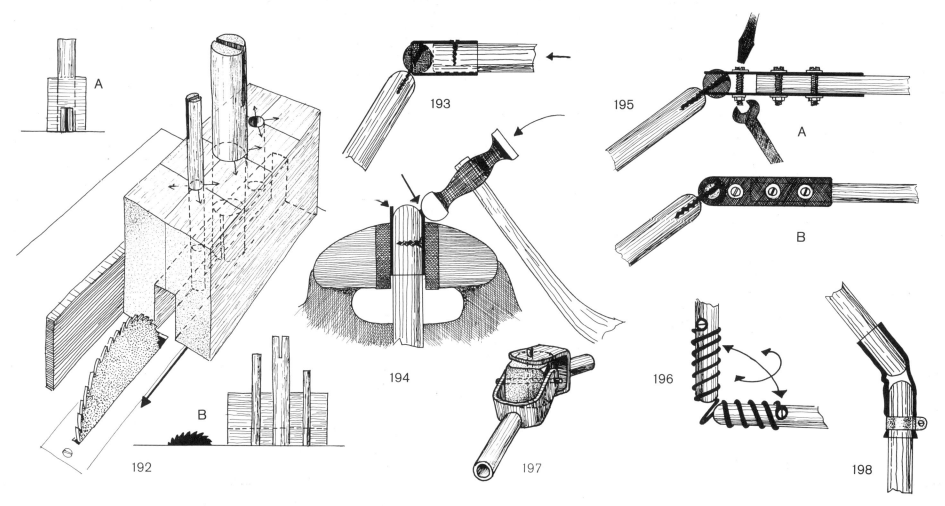

A

193

194

195

A

B

196

197

198

192

B

Then the dowel is removed and the iron or brass ball is inserted in its place. The ball should be drilled to take a screw so that it can be fixed to the top end of the upper arm. When that is done the appropriate end of the shoulder is fitted into the tube and fixed with a screw. Now the ball can turn without otherwise losing its position.

Figs. 195 A and 195 B show another ball-joint. A small square baton or a dowelstick is put beween two pieces of strip-iron and held in position by two bolts. A third bolt tightens the grip of these strips on the upper arm ball which rests in holes two thirds the size of the ball's diameter. The joint can be adjusted by tightening or loosening the third bolt.

Up till now we have only dealt with hinged joints and ball joints, but we must not forget the universal joint. Fig. 196 shows how a spring can work as a universal joint if it is secured in position with two screws. If the weight of the arm-pieces and the tension of the spring are suitable co-ordinated this spring-joint can also function like a hinged joint. Again, a piece of rubber tubing attach-ed to the arm-piece with tube-clamps can function as a universal joint, as demonstrat-ed in fig. 198. In 197 we see a universal joint proper. You can buy small versions of these cheaply in any model-building shop.

Most amateurs worry about how to make puppet hands. For one thing they are generally under the impression that it is easier to shape a head than to carve a hand. For another it worries them that a puppet needs not only one hand, but two: a difficult and laborious task. Undoubtedly carved hands are preferable to all other kinds of hands, that is, of course, if one knows how to carve them. There is no need to explain the problems to an experienced woodcarver, and the only advice I can give to the inexperienced is: keep on trying! Carving is a matter of feeling, artistic ability and experience. I am convinced that I cannot deal with these problems in a few lines, so I shall dismiss this attempt altogether. I shall, however, demonstrate a few possibilities of producing puppet hands in the following paragraphs.

For puppets made of fabric or from a stocking, fabric hands are, of course, most appropriate. For this purpose draw the shape of the hand on a wooden board (fig. 199). Then put pins along the line and afterwards remove the heads with a pair of pliers. Now bend a wire around this pattern. The wire should be of the strength that can just be bent by hand. Then cut two pieces of cloth the same shape as the pattern but adding an extra width for sewing. Cover the wire hand from both sides with a layer of cotton wool and then sew the whole thing between the fabric hands. It is best to fix the fabric to the wire in several places so that it cannot slide out of position when the hand is finally shaped in a gesture. It is easier, of course, to sew small gloves on a sewing machine and then turn them inside out and pad them with cotton wool. By sewing across the padded fingers at the joints you can even make the fingers moveable. But don't forget that small gloves are hard to turn inside out. You can also strengthen a normal glove hand by pushing wire into the fingers. The top of the wire should be bent to a small loop for this purpose.

I can well imagine that you ask yourself why all my puppet hands have only three fingers and a thumb. If there are only three fingers instead of four they are less fragile. Besides, I feel it does not matter if a puppet hand has three fingers, as long as it is well proportioned. A hand with three fingers is also simpler to look at and definitely simpler to make, and so I do without the fourth finger. These reasons are good enough for me; if it worries anybody, they are free to make puppet hands with four fingers! If an audience finds time to count the fingers during a performance, the puppeteer is not much good.

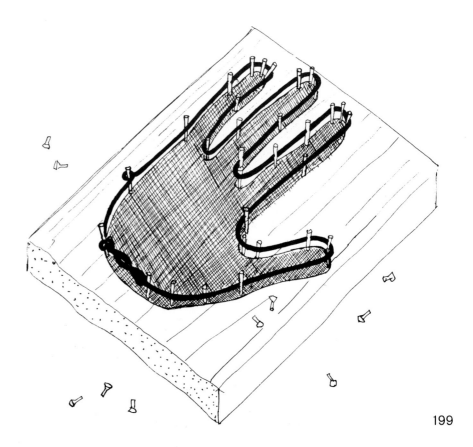

199

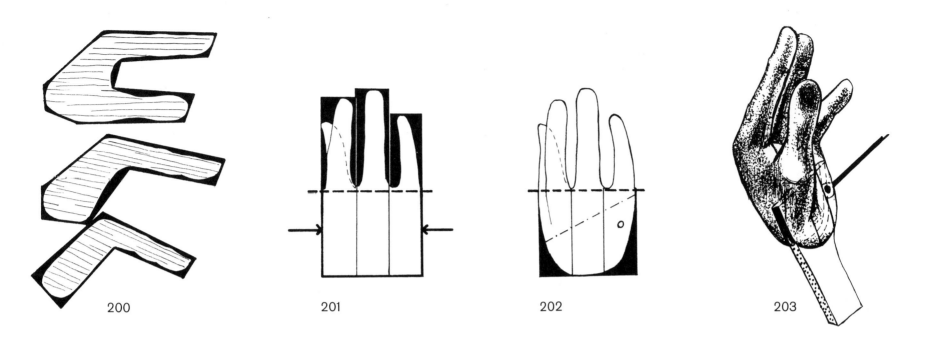

200   201   202   203

In figs. 200 to 203 you can see the production of a wooden hand composed of individual wooden sections. These hands have proved very efficient and are easy to make. First you make finger models from hardboard. After you have cut them out with a jigsaw or bandsaw you have to sand them down carefully so that you can use them as patterns. In fig. 200 the white shape indicates the hardboard pattern, the black outline shows the roughly cut wooden block of finger thickness. You should file down these hand sections to their drawn outlines. Then shape the part of the actual fingers with file and sandpaper. It would complicate matters considerably, if you put the hand together before filing down the fingers. When filing down the individual sections be aware of the shape of the hand as a whole. As soon as the front part of the fingers is completed, glue the pieces together with cold glue. As long as the glue has not yet set, you can still correct the shape of the hand by moving the sections. Thus you can give the hands the look which is most characteristic for the puppet they are made for. As soon as you have found their right position clamp the sections together at the lower end which has not yet been carved (see arrows in fig. 201).

In fig. 202 you see the final shape of the hand. The dotted line across the back of the hand indicates how far you can insert the leather joint and where to fasten the rod for manipulation. On the three dimensional drawing in fig. 203 you can see the strip of leather; it is narrower than the hand so that there is enough space in the slot for the wire loop of the rod as well. The wire loop is held in position by a pin or a screw. This method of manipulation leads to great accuracy and there is no danger of catching the fingers with the rod, but only hands made from strong wood or strong synthetic material can be operated in this way. For this kind of manipulation the hand has to be fixed to the arm in such a way that in its rest position the edge of the hand points downwards.

Although this description of making a puppet hand from single fingers may sound rather complicated, it is still the easiest and most effective wooden hand for any beginner or amateur to make.

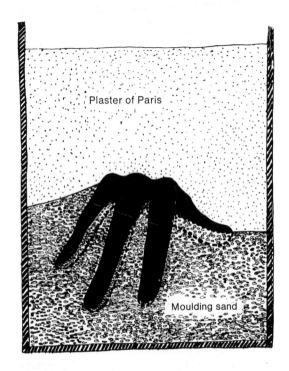

Plaster of Paris

Moulding sand

204

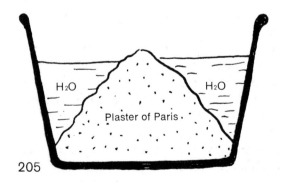

H₂O   H₂O

Plaster of Paris

205

It is a far more difficult task to make an accurate plaster of paris mould for a hand, as shown in fig. 204. This technique is only worthwhile if the mould is going to be used several times, or if heads or hands are to be made from rubber solution. You can of course use the same mould when working with synthetic resin, and in this case the work involved in making a mould is certainly justified.

1. As with the work with paper and glue, a master model from clay or plasticine has to be made. Both heads and hands can be made that way. It is, however, important to realise that a successful two part mould can only be made around a simple model. If the model has overlapping parts, the model (and later the cast) cannot be taken out of the mould, or parts of the plaster get caught in the model or cast. Therefore a mould for a complicated model must be made of several pieces.

2. Next you have to find a set of enclosing walls, well-glued cardboard can be used or wooden boards. These you need for holding together moulding sand and liquid plaster. The black and white margin on fig. 204 indicates this enclosure. Boards can be clamped, cardboard has to be carefully stuck or tied together. Make sure there is no leak either at the bottom or the corners. Another thing to remember is that this housing for the mould has to be very much higher than the model so that enough plaster can be poured over it to make a strong mould wall.

3. Now fill enough moulding sand into this housing to be able to bed the lower half of the model comfortably. Push the model into the sand till one half exactly sticks out. You can work more accurately with slightly moist sand, which has also the advantage of absorbing less water from the plaster. Once you have properly placed and bedded the model, clean the top half very carefully with a brush. With everything cleaned and checked you can start to prepare the plaster.

4. In fig. 205 you see a cross-cut of a bowl. First you fill the bowl with water till you are convinced that the quantity of the water plus plaster is sufficient to fill the space above the model, that is to say to be able to make a strong first half of the mould. When mixing plaster always put water into the bowl first, then pour the plaster carefully into the middle of the bowl till the top of a plaster hill appears above the surface of the water. Then stir plaster and water together thoroughly.

5. Before pouring the whole lot over the model, it is advisable to sprinkle some of it on to the model first, till it is totally covered with a thin layer. If you happen to know how long the plaster takes to set, it is good to pour it over the model when it is just about to thicken so that it sets as quickly as possible. You can only get the timing right by experimenting beforehand, as not every plaster sets at the same time. It is important that once poured the plaster sets quickly otherwise the cardboard gets soft or the liquid leaks. It is also important to make sure that the plaster mould has a smooth, flat surface, as this first half of the mould has to be turned upside down once the plaster has set.

6. After the plaster has set, remove the

housing and turn the model upside down. Then clear all the sand carefully from the lower — now upper — half of the model, for every grain of sand left on the model will be visible on the later cast. With a pointed knife or a spattle dig three holes 1-2 cm deep into three corners of the existing half of the mould. These three holes will help later on to line up the two halves of the mould.

7. As first and second mould-pieces would stick together, the first half has to be covered with a separating substance. For this purpose add a little water to soap (soap flakes) and stir till it turns to foamy paste. Paint this carefully onto the joining surface of the first mould half.

8. Again you have to put the housing around the mould piece and model. Make sure it does not leak.

9. Once all this is done you repeat what has been described under (5) and (6).

10. After the second half has been cast, you cautiously separate the two halves, remove the model and leave the mould to dry. The second half has three protruding knobs which fit into the three holes of the first half. But so long as the plaster is still even only slightly wet, these knobs are very fragile. Therefore do not go any further until the plaster is absolutely dry which may take several days.

11. If you want to make rubber hands, the mould can be used as soon as it is dry, but only if you have carefully removed the plasticine or clay of the master model. Rubber solution is not available in ordinary shops. You have to buy it direct from a firm and you have to know the name and number of the specific brand you need.

Don't forget to leave a hole to pour the rubber solution into the mould. Leave a hole at the wrist when making a hand, at the neck when making a head. For good results it is essential that the mould should be absolutely dry and clean inside. Only then can the plaster absorb part of the water contained in the rubber solution so that the required thin layer of rubber can form around the inside of the mould wall. After setting for 30 to 60 minutes this layer will have acquired sufficient thickness. The remainder of the rubber solution can be poured back into the tin and kept for future use. After a period of vulcanisation the hands can easily be taken out of the mould. They are of a whitish-yellow colour and, unfortunately, hard to paint. Therefore it is necessary to dye the rubber solution before pouring it into the mould[1].

This technique was originally introduced by Ernst Guenther Schmidt[2]. I have tried it and it works; yet I personally found the result not aesthetically pleasing and therefore did not pursue it any further.

The plaster moulds can, of course, be used for paper moulding as well. But for this purpose it needs special preparation. When it is dry you have to paint the inside several times with shellac varnish, you also have to paint the edge of the mould. The varnish fills the pores of the plaster and the surface becomes smooth and water-tight. As in paper moulding with a master model, layer after layer of paper has to be placed inside the mould. It is important, however, to use no paste for the first layer, this has to consist of moist paper only. Adhesion makes the wet paper cling to the mould. Only when the inside is completely covered can you start to use paste. If you use paste too early you will not be able to remove the papercast from the mould without damaging either the mould or the cast itself.

Another way of making fully modelled hands is by filling the mould with synthetic resin which will then consolidade. There are good handbooks available for the use of synthetic resin. If you want to avoid accidents and achieve satisfying results, it is best to obtain exact information about the particular product you want to use.

Moulds can also be made from resilient plastic products which for some time dental technicians have been using for dentures. The material however, is very expensive, so it is probably only worth using it for making resin hands. If you have someone from the dental profession among your friends he will probably be able to help you. Dentists have to work so accurately that their advice should be extremely useful. As I personally have no experience in that field, this can only remain a hint for possible exploration. As many artificial teeth are made from synthetic resin, there is no doubt that the technical possibilities are there (see footnotes at the back).

[1] Rubber dye in Germany from Siegle und Co. GmbH.; Farbenfabriken, Sieglestr. 25, 7 Stuttgart-Feuerbach.
[2] Essay in a specialist's magazine called *Perlicko-Perlacko,* edited by Dr. H. R. Purschke, Frankfurt am Main.

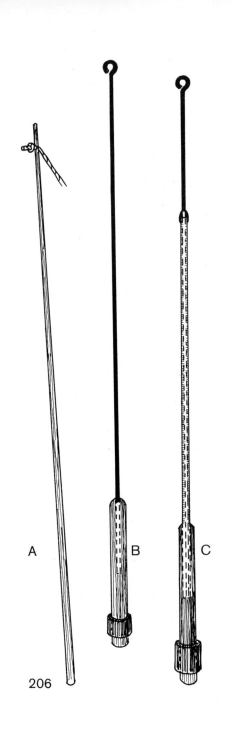

A

206

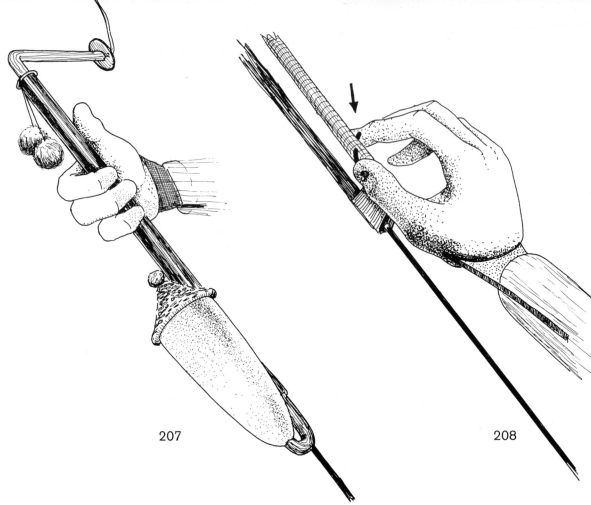

207

208

Figs. 206 A, B and C show three well-proved forms of manipulation rods. (A) is made from wood and it is the kind that is used with Javanese rod-puppets. You have to use tough and flexible wood or bamboo. The puppet hand is fixed to the rod with a piece of string.

In 206 (B) the rod is of high tensile steel with a piece of hardwood dowel for a handle. In order to make the handle less slippery a rubber ring is put around it at the bottom. A piece of rubber tubing will do. The upper end of the rod is bent to a loop. The lower end is slightly flattened (this is not visible on the drawing) and inserted into a very tight hole in the wood. Such a rod is very flexible and therefore not suitable for every puppet. If you want a more rigid rod, which yet has a certain amount of flexibility, the one shown in fig. 206 (C) would probably be the best one to use. The lower part of the steel rod is encased within a thin brass tube. Rod and tube are either glued together with a two component glue[1], or brazed. First the brass tube is fastened inside the handle, then the rod is covered thoroughly with the two component glue and pushed into the tube with a twisting action so that the inside of the tube gets covered with glue as well. When the glue is set, rod and tube are joined, but heating the brass tube to 100 °C. strengthens the glue considerably. You can buy this brass tubing in model shops; the available length is 1 m, enough for two manipulation rods. Usually the steel rods are used as shanks for model ships and the brass tubes as their bearings, and therefore rod and tube fit exactly. Don't buy steel wire in coils, as it is very hard to straighten out and difficult to push into the tube.

In figs. 207 and 208 you see again two ways of hidden manipulation of hands. Pipe and bow are extensions of the manipulation rod. A nylon string is fastened to the mouthpiece, as it was to the trumpet which we have discussed before. The string is threaded through the puppet's mouth. If you pull the string, the mouthpiece meets the mouth unfailingly, if you relax the string, you can manipulate the arm freely.

The hand of the violinist is loosely strung to the bow, again with a nylon thread (see arrow in fig. 208). If the arm, bow and string are cleverly placed in this manner, the puppet hand repeats the puppeteer's movements exactly. Rolf Trexler showed me the trick with his unique gypsy violinist, one of the most fascinating puppets I have ever seen. Glove and rod puppets usually don't have legs as they are worn like a glove over the hand and arm of the operator. The immediate contact the puppeteer enjoys by wearing the puppet as a glove would be lost and replaced by a tiresome mechanism, if we wanted to show the whole figure with legs all the time. If you do want to do this, it is undoubtedly wiser to use a string puppet. So far, to my mind, only Richard Teschner and the Japanese Bunraku Theatre have succeeded in making convincing rod puppets with legs. Only with certain exceptions do I feel this technical effort to be justified. Still, there are cases when we cannot do without legs, and therefore I will mention a few possible methods of constructing them. Let us talk about the glove puppet first. Kasperl usually has legs and so, sometimes, has his antagonist the Devil. As I believe that many of my readers have seen those dangling legs of Kasperl, I will not show them in a diagram here. One can remember the scene when Kasperl sits on the playboard with bent knees and straightens them out as if pushing himself backwards; or the occasions when Kasperl uses his leg as a truncheon. In this kind of leg it is usual to make the foot and lower part of the leg in one piece. At the knee the leg is fixed to a tube of fabric of the same kind as the costume. This tube is sewn to the costume at the appropriate height. When the legs are to appear, the puppeteer, using his second hand, operates them by moving the heels. If he does it well, it looks rather convincing.

A further development of this sort of leg is the one shown in fig. 209. The lower part of the leg is made of wood. The upper leg is a tube of thin wood or cardboard into which the puppeteer can put his fingers. A piece of leather is used for the knee joint. The hand that operates the legs is invisible as it is hidden by the costume.

209

[1] In Germany: UHU & AgomentU3 & hardener. In England: Aroldite.

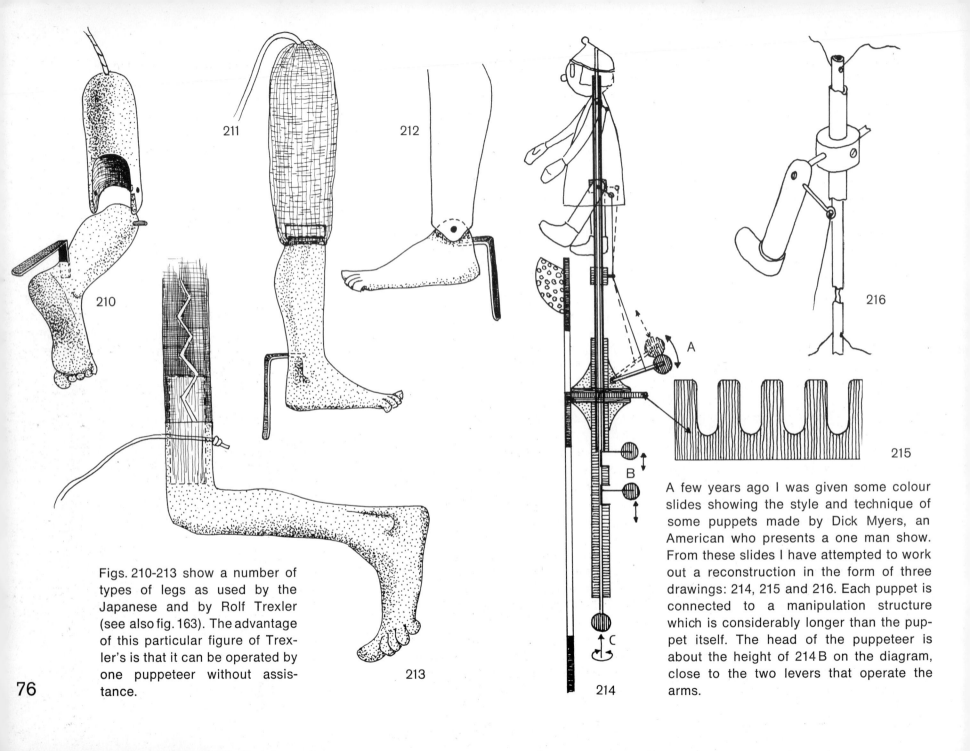

211

212

210

213

216

A

B

C

215

214

Figs. 210-213 show a number of types of legs as used by the Japanese and by Rolf Trexler (see also fig. 163). The advantage of this particular figure of Trexler's is that it can be operated by one puppeteer without assistance.

A few years ago I was given some colour slides showing the style and technique of some puppets made by Dick Myers, an American who presents a one man show. From these slides I have attempted to work out a reconstruction in the form of three drawings: 214, 215 and 216. Each puppet is connected to a manipulation structure which is considerably longer than the puppet itself. The head of the puppeteer is about the height of 214 B on the diagram, close to the two levers that operate the arms.

The manipulation structure consists of the following parts:

1. A cylinder of wood 8-10 cm in diameter is drilled through lengthwise. Running through inside this is a long piece of wooden dowel. This dowel holds the head at the top, goes right through the tube and has a wooden ball at its lower end (214 C). Rod and ball move the head. Instead of the dowel you could use another metal tube which would extend the possibility of movement. Two wooden discs are glued around the top third of the wooden cylinder. Their distance apart corresponds to the thickness of the playboard (215). The dotted substance which holds the levers for manipulating the legs, consists of plastic wood.

2. Along that part of the metal tubing which protrudes from the wooden cylinder, three gadgets guide the strings for manipulating arms and legs. These three points of control are invisible to the audience. The lowest is covered by the footlights and the two higher ones by the costume.

3. This rather big structure carries a relatively small puppet. Its head is made from a wooden ball and so is its nose. The body is funnel-shaped and made from plastic wood. Legs and arms, which have no joints, are made from the same material, and they can only move back and forth like those of a jumping jack or a mechanical figure. The head has a slot at the neck so that it can nod and turn. On fig. 216 you can see the leg mechanism once again, but this time as a perspective drawing. The strings always run through tubing or grooves.

This puppet can only turn around by moving its whole body and it cannot bend at all. If one considers the pros and cons of such a puppet, one wonders whether the sacrifice of the direct contact between puppeteer and puppet (and with that a great number of possibilities of movement) is justified by the visibility of a pair of artificially moving legs which might be, but are not necessarily, funny.

I have devoted so much space to this puppet, because I know how often one's sense of perfecting puppets makes one miss the right path. I myself have often been led astray, therefore I want to warn you that it is easy to waste time with misguided efforts. A short time before the publication of this English version of my book I had an opportunity to see two performances by Dick Myers. Both were excellent and received enthusiastic audience response. The puppets, which are rather stiff to my way of thinking, became incredibly lively and amusing through their creator's inspired way of presentation and brilliant manipulation. This apparent contradiction goes to show that it is the puppeteer's power of animation that makes a puppet convincing on stage; the puppet itself is only his instrument. But I would discourage any inexperienced puppeteer from using Dick Myers' technique, because to do so would emphasise any weaknesses he might have.

Before we talk about heads and their mechanics here are a few drawings which show in detail some simple devices which you can make yourself for transmitting and directing power.

In fig. 217 you see a simple gadget for moving the head. The piece of rubber (from a motor car inner tube) is screwed to the hidden shoulder-piece. The simple see-saw movement on 218 is a device for effective head movement or for the alternate movement of legs.

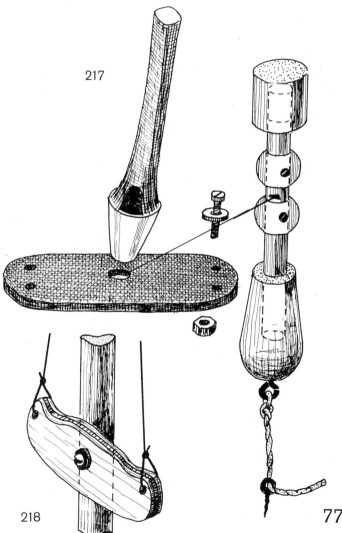

217

218

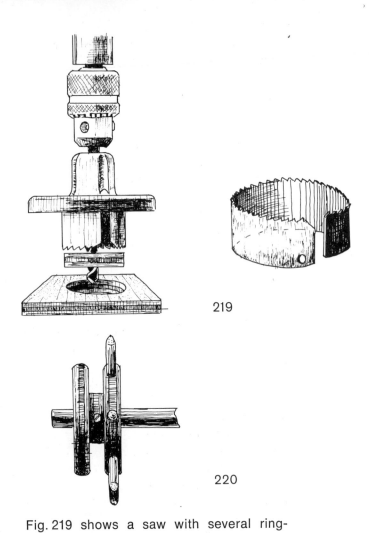

219

220

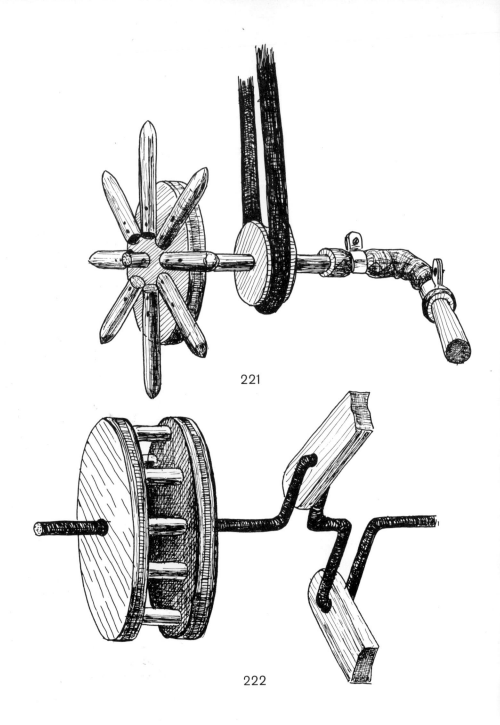

221

222

Fig. 219 shows a saw with several ring-shaped saw blades. With these you can easily and quickly cut wooden discs of varying sizes. The saw is available in tool and hardware shops and is not expensive. Cogwheels, wheels for driving belts, crankshafts and connecting rods are often needed, but are difficult to find in the correct size. So here are a few suggestions for making them (figs. 219-222).

78

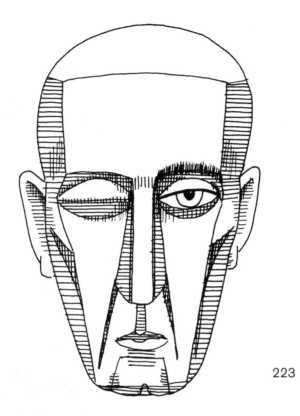

223

Let us begin by investigating the effect of light and shade on a face. This is of greater importance than the actual colours of the face as these can usually be created by coloured lighting.

The drawing of the head in fig. 223 is divided purposely into distinct, sharp-edged areas. Drawing a face in this manner shows which parts are seen from the front and which from the side, and it also shows us where there are recesses in the face. In fig. 223 the front view areas are left white, the side view areas lightly shaded and the recesses heavily shaded. With normal stage lighting, that is to say with overhead and front lighting, one achieves the effect shown in the diagram.

So it is important not to paint areas of shade too light, or frontal areas or protruding parts of the face too dark, as a mistake in this respect neutralises the effect of features and renders a face flat and expressionless. If the light and shade areas are treated as in our drawing 223, that is to say the front view areas especially light, and the recesses especially dark, then the effect, will be that of a striking, well defined face. A good puppet make-up usually consists of four shades:

1. A light shade of the basic colour of the face usually applied over all as a first coat.
2. A darker shade of the same colour, or some suitable other colour, for all the non-front view areas.
3. An even darker shade of the same colour for the recesses in the face.
4. A very light shade for the front view areas and highlights. Such highlights are on the

CHAPTER VII

The Head

The colouring, or rather the make-up of a puppet's face is of greater importance than is usually assumed. The make-up emphasises the three dimensional effect of the head, brings out the characteristics of the face, and where necessary, covers up unintentional irregularities on the surface. When painting a puppet head the effect on it of coloured stage lights should be taken into consideration. Pink, for instance, looks grey and colourless in a green light.

ridge of the nose, on the cheek bones, the chin, the lower lip, on the lateral edges of the forehead, and sometimes on protruding areas of the eyelids.

Refer to the painted part of fig. 224 for an illustration of the above. The intermediate shades — which we have not yet discussed — function as transitions between contrasting areas. These intermediate shades, however, can also be used for the purpose of emphasising parts of the face; by using them for the upper lip, for instance, the lightly painted tip of the nose becomes even more apparent.

The whole colour scheme on fig. 224 is based on pink. This pink, however, is not just a simple combination of any red with white, but is a pink of varying shades: shades of dark, cool pink to warm, orange pink — from pale pink to dark ochre and brown. The very dark areas are painted with unmixed Bordeaux red, but could also be purple.

Looking at the head from a certain distance the impression is of a colour that is a mixture of pink and yellow, a colour combination which gives the face a leathery quality, well suited to its hard, unscrupulous, strong-willed, clever expression. These characteristics are emphasised by the deep lines between nose and mouth and the hollow cheeks which are also a feature of his age. This gentleman would look younger and less grim if he were not bald but had a full complement of dark hair.

With the colours shown on the chart below figs. 225 and 226 any puppet face can be painted.

When painting a puppet head it is advisable to start with a coat of white poster paint, because this gives the colours to be applied later a greater intensity.

The method of painting a face as shown in fig. 224 is also observed in figs. 225 and 226, except that the basic colour is a dark pink. It may be mixed with carmine, madder lake or Bordeaux red, which are used in the human theatre for making up old faces.

For making up young people or children one has to use warmer shades of red like vermilion or perhaps some orange.

Just as the shape of the face of a puppet has to be somewhat exaggerated to be effective on stage, so it is with the painting of the face. The naturalistic colours of a human being should not be imitated when painting a puppet. The make-up of a puppet has to be strongly emphasised with exaggerated contrasts and highlights.

Referring to the optical illusions colours can create, a painter will tell you that colours have different space values. To illustrate the meaning of this try the following simple experiment: take four coloured discs of equal size, one yellow, one red, one blue and one green, and hang them at an equal distance from one another on a wall. Then step back to look at them and you will observe an unexpected phenomenon; the yellow plate will seem to hover in front of the wall and the blue plate to be behind it or beyond it. Only the red and green discs will appear to be at the right distance from you. The conclusion to be drawn from this is that warm coloured things appear to be nearer than those which are painted with cold colours.

The same applies when we consider the intensity of colours. The stronger a colour, the more captivating it is to the eye, while pale colours, on the other hand, always assume a background quality. From these facts we can draw the following conclusions:

1. Unmixed colours stand out in the foreground (by unmixed colours we mean colours not mixed with black, white or grey, which have a neutralising effect on them).
2. Mixed and pale colours are unobtrusive.
3. Warm colours such as yellow or vermilion seem closer to the observer than cold colours such as blue.

Bearing these rules in mind not only can you paint puppet faces effectively but also, by using the quality of optical illusion of certain colours as discussed above, you can cover up weaknesses in the structure of a face. In other words the appearance of a shape can be altered by painting.

As I indicated before, the simplest solution to a problem is usually preferable to a complicated one. This is particularly true where the facial expression of a puppet is concerned. I had to come to grips with the problem when I was given the task of designing and making a set of five puppets to represent Kasper, a witch, Mephistopheles, Sherlock Holmes and a professor of physics. These puppets were supposed to have a great deal of expression but at the same time be technically simple, preferably with no mechanical devices for facial movement.

At about this time there was an exhibition of the work of some art schools in Stuttgart. Amongst them was a set of string puppets

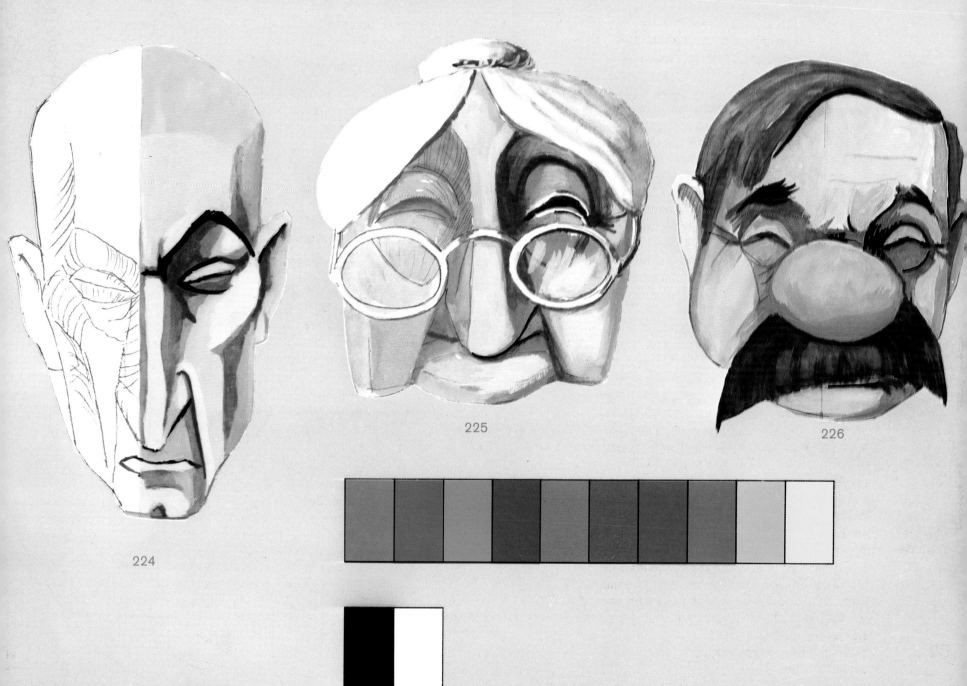

224

225

226

which were to have a great influence on my approach to the task I had undertaken. The puppets on exhibition were designed and made by a team from the Werkakademie Kassel under the supervision of Professor Roettger. They were mainly abstract figures. The purpose of the exercise was to demonstrate the functions of the law of proportion, of the pendulum, of movement and of equilibrium. The team gave a performance with these puppets and hung them up afterwards for the audience to inspect and handle. All these puppets were extremely sensitive and reacted to the slightest touch. According to their respective constructions they either started to walk, prance, dance or hop. The puppet heads were not made to represent human likeness. They were harmonious composites of convex and concave shapes supplemented with small spheres and rods according to the purpose of the exercise. These figures were made entirely of wood, beautifully and accurately constructed, and their joints were visible as they were neither painted nor costumed. Although they had no apparent similarity to human shapes, they were most intriguing symbols of people. I felt that something very essential and peculiar to puppetry had been realised in these puppets and in their performance.

As I said in my introduction, I do not think that puppets of this kind are suitable for performances in ordinary comedy or drama. They are more closely related to ballet. They are in their element with movement and dance but they are not for action or plot. I thought that these puppets were highly

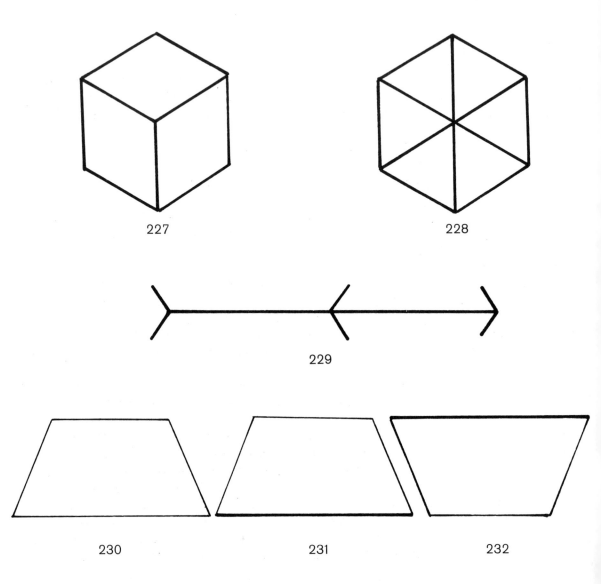

227

228

229

230

231

232

82

artistic and I found them to be as inspiring to my own work as the sculpture of, say, Henry Moore.

Subsequently I tried to integrate some aspects of the formal and optical illusion of these puppets into my own style without losing the physical and psychological characteristics of my figures. I tried to obtain a variety of expressions on a face without making it mechanically mobile.

Before going on, however, I want to say a few more things about optical illusion. Not only do colours sometimes play tricks on our eyes, but shapes also can have similar effects. When and to what degree our eyes are deluded depends on our visual habits. We cease to notice consciously the things which we have around us every day; we no longer react to them. When we become accustomed to driving a car, for instance, we cease to make conscious decisions when gear changing, accelerating or braking; we react automatically and do not think which foot has to be used on the accelerator and which on the brake pedal. The same is true when we look at scenes with which we are completely familiar. Our eyes are trained to differentiate between subtle nuances of colour, proportion and outline, but if a person becomes too accustomed to seeing a certain object or scene his mind does not consciously fully register what is before him. Therefore, just looking and conscientiously observing are two very different actvities. The well known examples illustrated in figs. 227-232 have some bearing on the matter.

Depending on the way you look at, or rather adjust your eyes to look at figs. 227 and 228, you can recognise in them a two-dimensional hexagon or a three-dimensional cube, but fig. 227 could also be interpreted as showing three sides of a hollow cube from below, and looking at 228 we could imagine it to be a hexagonal pyramid seen from above evenly lit from all sides. In fig. 229 the two lengths shown are equal, measure them if you don't believe it.

It is also very interesting to realise how a trapezoid can be interpreted as a perspective view of a rectangle when its upper or lower edge is emphasised as in figs. 231 and 232.

When I made the witch shown in fig. 233 I managed for the first time to integrate my own style of work with the new ideas which came to me as a result of the exhibition. I started by making a simple convex shape for the head. Then I carved two holes on either side of the nose till they met behind it, thus making a kind of connecting tunnel behind the nose, and against the back of this 'tunnel' I glued a piece of mirror. This mirror catches the light and reflects it according to the angle and direction in which the puppet is looking, and in this way every now and again light is flashed into the audience. If the witch is seen in profile, the mirror effect is lost, but the tunnel behind the nose becomes visible and creates the illusion of an eye. If this puppet is well manipulated, that is to say if the mirror effect is cleverly used, the facial expression changes constantly although her face has no moving parts. A hunched back, spider-like hands and a flapping headscarf complete the spooky appearance of the puppet. In fact it turned out to be a rather frightening figure, and we were careful not to show her to very small children lest she should give them nightmares.

You can easily imagine how difficult it is to operate such a puppet effectively. It can only be done well if each movement of the puppet is plotted by the director from the viewpoint of the audience.

By working with this ensemble of puppets I came to the conclusion that convex shapes can be associated with wicked and macabre characters and with this discovery in mind I started working on a new set of puppets for the Threepenny Opera (234, 236, 237).

The Beggar shown in fig. 234 is painted and costumed in different shades of grey. He is bald, has hollow cheeks, and a mean and suspicious nature, and has an uncanny way of scrutinising anyone who looks at him. Like the witch he has behind his nose a 'tunnel' which looks like an eye when his head is seen in profile. In full face the white frontal area of the eye catches the light effectively. Fig. 235 is a separate drawing of such an eye. I put a cube inside half an ellipsoid, painted the inside and the front of the cube white, and the sides of the cube and 2—3 mm at each edge of the front I painted black. These black sides represent the iris and pupil of the eye. Depending on the angle from which the face is seen, the pupil appears to be either large or long and narrow, like a cat's eye. In front of the receding mouth, chin and nose seem to meet like a clamp, and with the play of light and shade the illusion of a chewing or mumbling movement is created.

84

233   234   235

Peachum, the beggar king, fig. 236, is an avaricious, mean old man with a trembling, silky, yellow goat's beard. His eyes, which seem to pop out of their eye sockets, are made of small pieces of hardwood dowel. They straighten up automatically when the puppet lifts his head and it is only then that iris and pupil are seen. These are painted on the top ends of the dowels and this gives the eyes a piercing expression. When the puppet looks downwards the pupils are not seen and the expression on his face appears to be pensive and drowsy. All in all he looks the really disagreeable character he is supposed to be.

The same can be said of his wife (fig. 237). Her malicious face is painted pea-green and the edges round her sockets white. She has an emaciated body with low drooping breasts, made with paper and glue over a plasticine model. She wears a tight fitting purple velvet dress with a high collar which looks prim and rather old-fashioned and reflects her virtuous pretensions. In keeping with the puppet's other characteristics her hands are long and narrow.

Her eyes are made of two shiny metal discs which are screwed to a strip of rubber. With two pieces of string the rubber is loosely fastened to the inside of the socket and held in position by another piece of string crossing to the back of the head. Thus the eyes are given constant yet limited amount of free movement. So you see the illusion of a mobile puppet face can be created without complicated and risky mechanical gadgets.

236

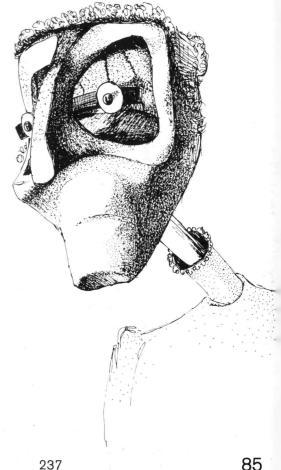

237

85

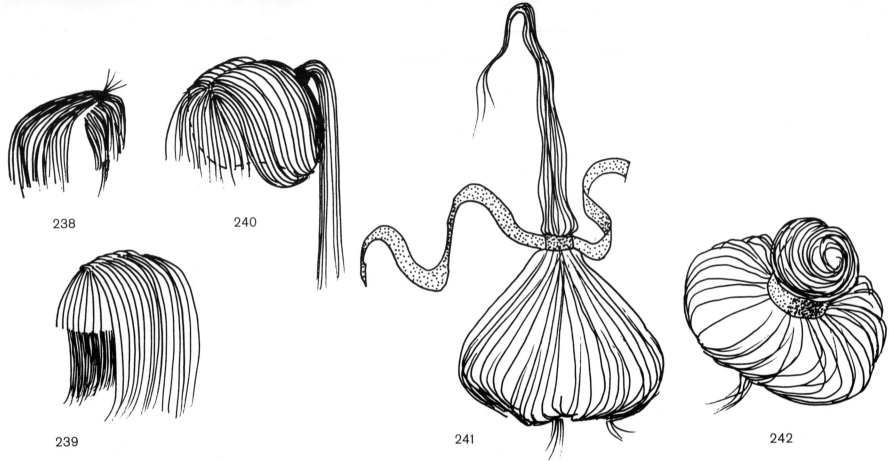

238

240

239

241

242

Hairstyles and wigs and the methods by which they are made are important as they can change the looks of a puppet completely. The usual materials for puppet wigs are wool, raffia, string, hemp, wire, bristles, steel wool, saucepan cleaners etc. I personally do not recommend human hair or fur as they tend to look too naturalistic on a puppet for my liking, although a person with great artistic ability might use them effectively in special cases. I would not declare the use of fur as forbidden, but I myself have never used it since my first and very uncertain

attempts at making puppets.

The usual way of fastening a wig to a head is by gluing it on with Bostik. With cloth or stocking puppets, however, it is better to sew the wig to the head rather than to glue it. The same applies to wire or steel wool wigs which, in any case, cannot be glued. Removable wigs are made by sewing or gluing the hair on to a tight-fitting skull cap.

Figs. 238-242 show three simple hairstyles for puppets representing young people, and one for an old lady. It is important to main-

tain the same density of hair throughout the wig. It should be glued in tufts to the scalp. A method of gluing on hair is shown in figs. 243 and 244. The ends of the hair are glued on to the head in the opposite direction to which the hair itself will ultimately be combed. When the glue has set it should be combed to the correct side. In a case such as the one shown in fig. 244 where the wig belongs to a fellow with scanty hair, it is not effective to glue the whole length of the hair to the head. Glue it, as indicated, to the head at its roots and comb it later into its proper

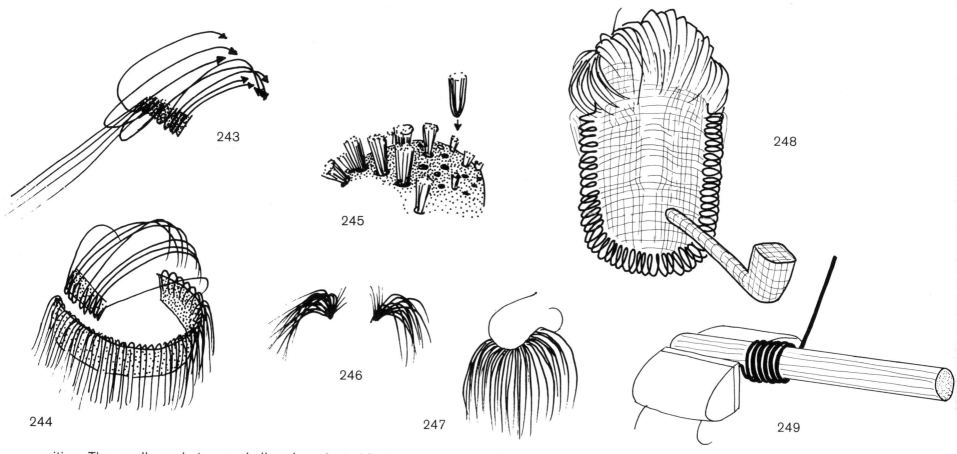

243

245

248

244

246

247

249

position. The small gap between skull and hair and the possibility for it to move when the puppet is operated, gives the wig the quality and effect of hair which a glued down immobile mat does not possess. In cases where it can be predicted that the hair will get out of position during the performance, it is an idea to fasten some of the ends to the head with a dab of Bostik.

Making the bristle wig shown in fig. 245 is more laborious. Holes (not in straight lines) are drilled into the skull and these are half-filled with glue. Tufts of bristles are then planted in them one by one. Once the tufts are firmly fixed, the bristles can be clipped to the desired shape with a pair of sharp scissors, just as a gardener clips his hedge. As it is not possible to plant the bristles too densely, it is advisable to paint the skull the same colour as the bristles before putting them in.

Eyebrows also are usually fastened to the face in tufts (see fig. 246).

Moustaches look fuller and more impressive if they are fastened directly under the nose rather than on the upper lip, (see fig. 247).

I once had to make a narrow, curly beard for a puppet representing a painter (248). For this purpose I wound wire around a hardwood dowel as in fig. 249. I threaded each end of the spiral so formed through the puppet's temples and bent the wire ends in such a way that they could no longer slip out. Using a bent saddler's needle I 'sewed' the lower part of the beard to the face in three places. This puppet's wig was made of silky fringes but somehow the two very different qualities of 'hair' did not clash.

Talking about beards and moustaches, I remember a short number that I once devised for covering up a scene change or for introducing a variety programme. I decided to make a Prussian military band. The head of the trumpeter was to be of such a size that a puppeteer could slip his hand inside it (see figs. 250 and 251). I thought it would be funny to give the trumpeter a revolving moustache which could be twirled around at appropriate moments during the performance. I cut out the shape of the moustache in plywood which I built up with sacking and glue and then covered with threads of wool. I drilled a hole into the trumpeter's upper lip and re-inforced it from the inside with a rubber disc with a hole punched through the middle. I fixed the moustache to a piece of hardwood dowel and pushed it through the hole in the upper lip. To operate the moustache, I fixed a small toggle to the inner end of the dowel, this also served the purpose of stopping the dowel from slipping back through the hole again. With this control one could not only twirl the moustache, but also lift and lower it. When the ends of the moustache pointed downwards the puppet looked sad and when they pointed upwards, he looked perky. These effects were, however, not quite enough to make him a really interesting puppet, so as an added attraction I made his spiked helmet movable. To do this I cut a hole into the trumpeter's skull and inserted a handle for the helmet. With my index finger I could now operate the helmet, that is to say, I could make it fall forwards over the puppet's eyes and pull it back again. With thumb and

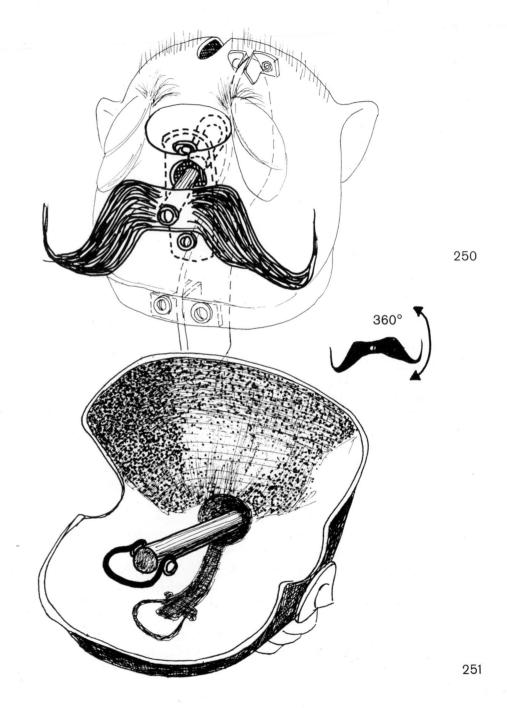

250

360°

251

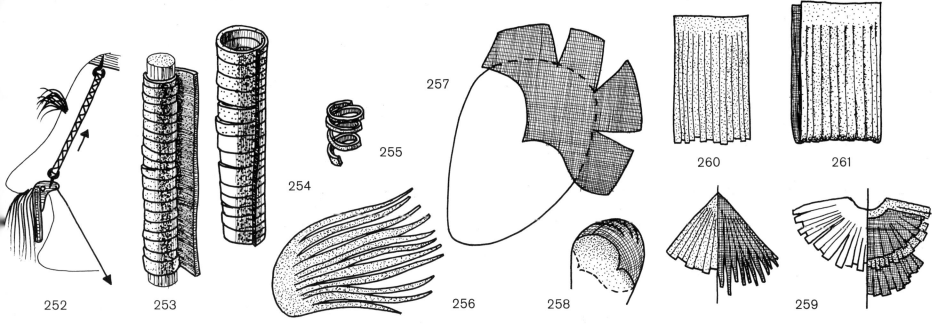

252 253 254 255 257 256 258 259 260 261

middle finger I manipulated the moustache. As most of my fingers were occupied with manipulating these various parts I had to support the puppet and hold it steady by means of a special piece of plywood shaped to my hand. It rested between the middle and index fingers on my palm and was pressed against the base of my thumb by my third and little fingers.

Another way of making a moustache wobble is shown in fig. 252. Again the single hairs are fixed to a piece of plywood. The piece of rubber keeps it in its normal position and the string operates it.

Felt is a very suitable material for costumes as well as for wigs. With small puppets, especially stop-frame puppets for film or television, good results can be obtained by gluing the felt straight on to the body. This gives the impression of a well-fitting garment.

Figs. 253 to 261 show a number of different ways of making wigs with felt. Glue or sew the top parts of the pieces on to the head and leave the fringes hanging free. The more layers you use, the more dense the wig will be. Ringlets are best sewn to a wig and held in position with a few dabs of Bostik. If a stiff wig is required ordinary starch should be used on the felt. Soak the felt fringes in starch, wind them round a dowel of the required ringlet diameter and leave them to dry on the dowel. I cannot really give any more specific instructions as, after all, each puppet has to be decorated according to its own design and purpose and according to the maker's inventive ability and taste.

Usually when a task is finished a fresh and more difficult one will present itself. Every project completed breeds new aims and ambitions and it is, therefore, quite natural that at a certain stage of our puppet-making career we should want to experiment with technically advanced mechanism. This has happened to me and some of my experiments have turned out well and others not so well. On certain issues I compared notes with ideas published in professional puppeteer's magazines and compared the results given with those I had obtained myself. From amongst these experiments I have selected some which I think successful and which I will discuss here. Many of the solutions to technical problems are common knowledge amongst professionals and it is often difficult to say who was initially responsible for an idea. But wherever I am able to give credit I will of course do so.

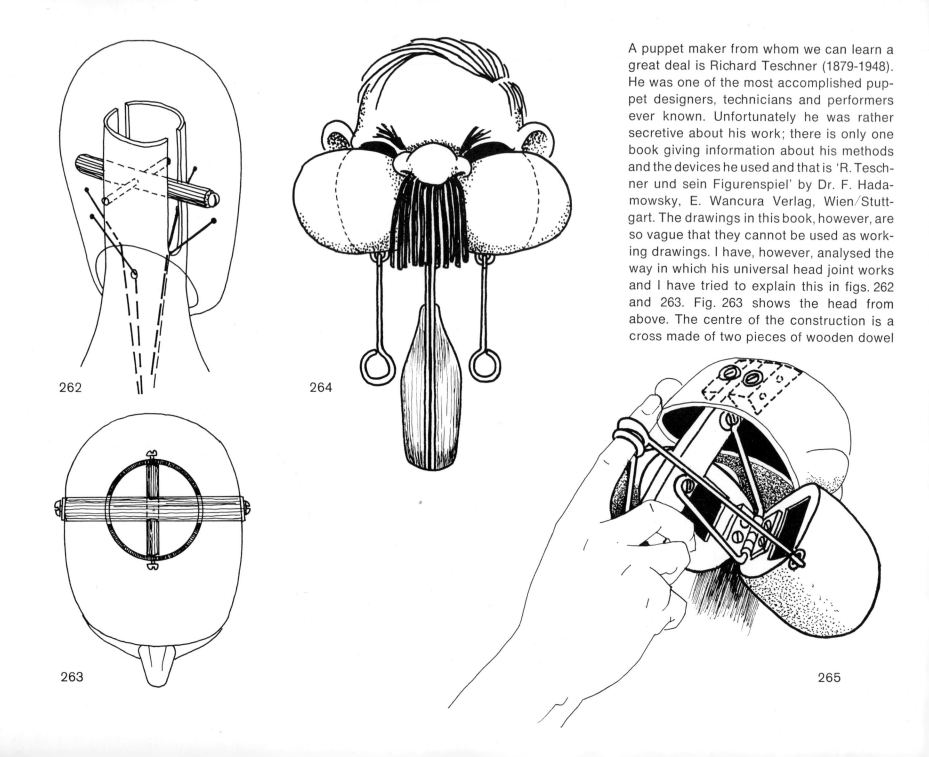

262

264

263

A puppet maker from whom we can learn a great deal is Richard Teschner (1879-1948). He was one of the most accomplished puppet designers, technicians and performers ever known. Unfortunately he was rather secretive about his work; there is only one book giving information about his methods and the devices he used and that is 'R. Teschner und sein Figurenspiel' by Dr. F. Hadamowsky, E. Wancura Verlag, Wien/Stuttgart. The drawings in this book, however, are so vague that they cannot be used as working drawings. I have, however, analysed the way in which his universal head joint works and I have tried to explain this in figs. 262 and 263. Fig. 263 shows the head from above. The centre of the construction is a cross made of two pieces of wooden dowel

265

90

of different thickness. The thinner piece is the shorter of the two and is loosely fitted with screws through two holes in the neck so that it can twist freely. The neckpiece has slots at the sides so that the thicker, longer dowel can see-saw freely on the fulcrum of the thinner piece which supports it. The length of the long cross-dowel corresponds to the width of the head. The thin piece is fixed to the neck in the same way as the long piece is fixed to the head. In other words the heads is hung from the long piece with the aid of a screw at each end, and can therefore move forwards and backwards. The thin, short piece allows the head to move from side to side. Four strings control the movement (see 262).

In the Prussian brass band mentioned earlier we also had a tuba player, whose face and head mechanism is shown in figs. 264 and 265. It was important to demonstrate clearly how hard the player had to blow. At first I thought I could solve the problem by building inflatable balloons into the cheeks. I was afraid, however, they might burst at the wrong moment, so I thought of another idea. I wanted him to look something like the drawing in fig. 264, the dotted line indicating the normal width of his cheeks and the outer line the inflated cheeks when he blew his instrument.
First, using paper and glue, I made and covered a model of the upper part of the head including the nose. Then I made a model that looked very much like a huge white bean, cut it in half and covered it with paper and glue. To the back of the skull I

fixed a pistol grip to which in turn I fastened a bent piece of wire. This functioned as the axle to a hinge which connected the two halves of the 'bean', as shown in fig. 265. Two little wire rods with fingerloops for the index finger made the cheeks operable. The smaller wire loops at the other ends of the rods were fixed to the back of the cheeks with nylon string. A moustache conceals the hinge from the front. The head opening at the back was not visible to the audience, as the puppet had a broad, high hunched back which, by the way, was also made by the method of modelling and then covering the model with glue and paper.

It is not easy to make puppet eyes that have the same range of movement as human eyes. Usually a puppet has either eyelids that can open and close, or rolling eyeballs, or eyes that can look from side to side.
In fig. 266 puppet eyes are shown that can be made to look from side to side only. The eyes pivot on two wood screws fastened to a dowel stick. A wire pin with a loop at the end projects from the back of each eyeball. The loops at the ends of these pins are held apart by another wire with a loop at each end allowing free simultaneous side to side movement. Two pieces of string which are attached to the wire loops, are threaded through a screw-eye inside each temple, led down through the neck and are then fastened to a rocker which completes the control system. If it is desired to include a mechanism which will pull the eyes back into their normal position, a rubber band correctly fastened will do the trick.

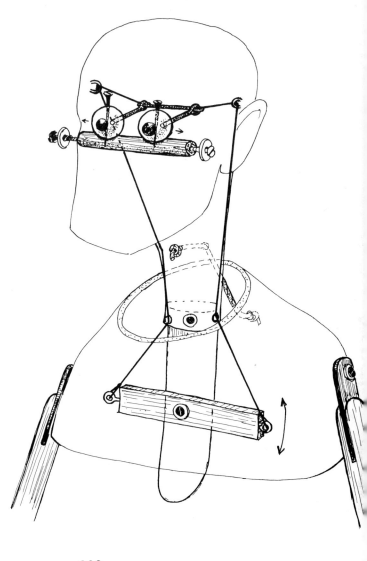

266

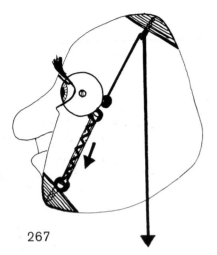

267

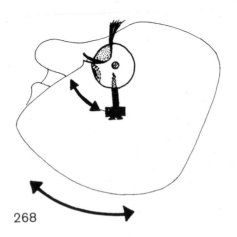

268

In fig. 267 both eyeballs are threaded on to a horizontal cross bar, which runs through the head. The backs of the balls are firmly connected to each other by another cross bar, and a string fixed to the centre of this bar and led through a screw-eye inside the top of the skull, is pulled from below to make the eyes look up and down. A rubber band attached to eyeballs and chin pulls the eyes back into their normal position. For emphasis eyelashes can be glued directly on to the eyeballs.

The eyes in fig. 268 are very similar in construction to the ones in 267, but they are made to open and close. They can be connected by a common bar which is weighted, or they can be weighted individually. In either case they can be made to appear to open and close by rocking the head backwards and forwards while the weight keeps the eyeballs at a fixed angle of vision.

Rolling eyes as in figs. 269 and 270 are not quite so easy to make as the previous ones, as they consist of several parts which have to be made with a considerable amount of skill.

The parts are:

1. Eyeballs consisting of segments of a wooden ball.
2. Axles made from hardwood dowel.
3. Wooden bobbins and string.
4. Elastic for pulling eyes back into normal position (not shown in the drawing) — optional.

Each eye axle runs into a bearing drilled into a block fastened to the back of the head. A heavy dowel is drilled out at appropriate points to form forward bearings. This is fas-

P

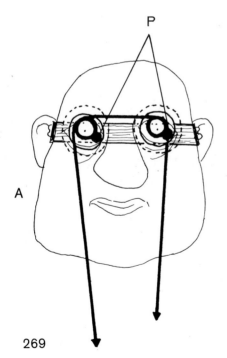

A

269

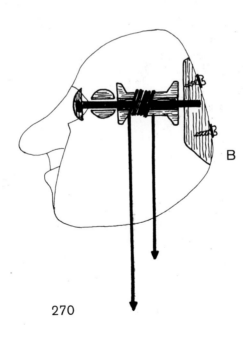

B

270

tened across the head behind the eyeballs. Eyeballs and bobbins are glued to the axles leaving enough space between bobbins and bearings to enable the axles to turn freely. If the relative proportions of the parts are correct, and the glue properly set, the eyes should no longer be able to drop out of the head.

A string brought up through the neck of the puppet, wound several times tightly around the first and then the second bobbin and brought back down again through the neck makes the eyes roll either left or right, as required. It is, of course, important to remember not to paint the pupils into the centre of the iris but off-centre (parallel to each other), otherwise the whole complicated mechanism would be ineffectual. 'P' in fig. 269 indicates where the pupils should be.

Spectacles are best made from wire. The easiest method is to make them of two separate parts as shown in fig. 271. One piece of wire makes up the whole frontal frame of the glasses, and another the two side pieces, which are connected to each other through the puppet's head. This way of attaching the glasses to the puppet has two advantages:

1. The glasses cannot get lost.
2. The puppet can easily toss them backwards, or, by nodding, flick them back on to its nose again.

If you decide that you want to attach your puppet's glasses in this way, it is best to reinforce the two holes you have drilled through the head with washers. If you omit this re-inforcement, you run the risk of getting the holes enlarged and torn with use.

For the pince-nez shown on fig. 273 you need only one piece of wire, the ends of which you push into the back of the puppet's nose.

A spectacle frame can of course also be made from plywood with the aid of a jigsaw. Perspex is an appropriate material for the glasses themselves, practicable, however, only if used in conjunction with a supporting wire frame.

273

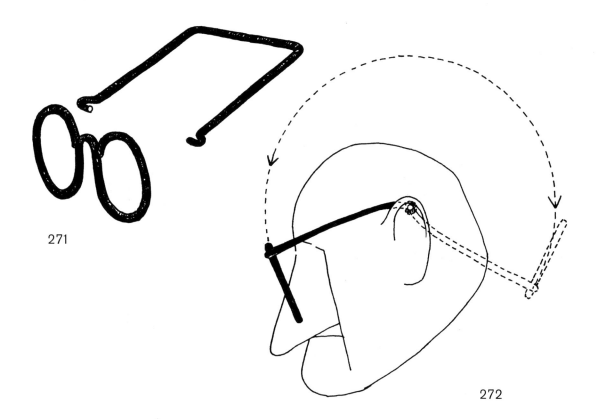

271

272

93

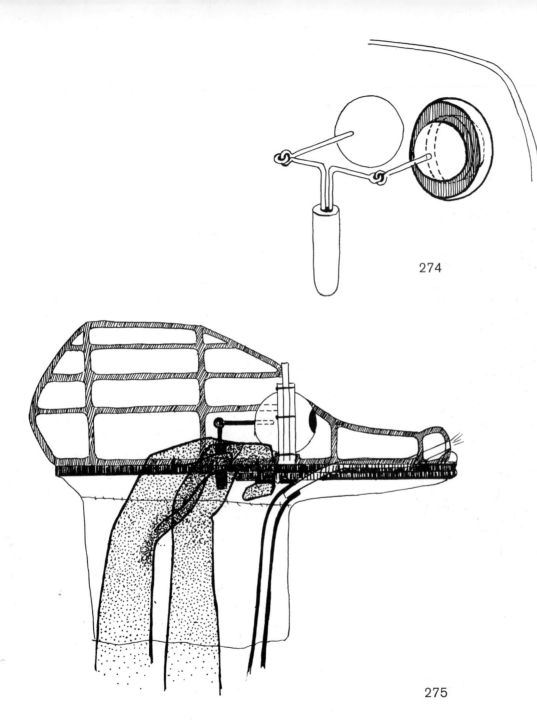

274

275

My later art teacher Theodor Schueck from my school in Freiburg devised what seems to me to be the simplest and most mobile puppet eye I have ever come across. At school he had set up a puppet stage where, every winter, plays written by himself or by other authors were performed. Amongst his plays (which he wrote under the pseudonym of Alexander Pepusch) was one which had the so-called 'brass bug' as a character. This brass bug rolled his eyes frighteningly, blew steam from his nostrils and devoured anything and everything which was made of metal. He also changed his size drastically during the show. His head and mechanism are seen in figs. 274, 275 and 276. The mechanism of the eye control and manipulation is so obvious from fig. 274 that little explanation is needed. The part that is not quite clear is the bearing of the eyeball. This is illustrated in 275 where it can be seen that the bearing consists of three pieces of wood with holes of varying diameter to keep the ball in place. The two outside pieces have a slightly smaller hole and thus keep the ball safely inside the middle ring. The puppeteer can move the handle of the eye control in any required direction.

Smoke was blown through the brass bug's nostrils with two tubes, his legs were cloth sausages which dangled loosely on strings from the body. The puppet is now between 35 and 40 years old and has found its way into the Munich Stadtmuseum, Jakobsplatz 1. This museum, by the way, contains the largest puppet collection in the world. It houses an incredible treasure of every sort and kind of puppet from every part of the

276

world. It also has a number of puppet stages and an extensive library of books on puppetry. Whether your interests in puppetry are historical, professional or merely those of curiosity, you are always welcome there to look at, study and even handle the puppets. It is not possible within the limits of this book to illustrate every detail of puppet mechanism and I therefore refer you back to figs. 121, 126, 146, 156, and 158 for the mechanisms for puppet mouths. With the mechanical possibilities we have discussed so far, and with a little imagination, the dedicated puppet-maker should now be able to make any glove or rod puppet he likes, even a horse and rider or horse and cart. The movement of the horse's legs and the cart's wheels can be synchronised and kept moving on the spot whereas the landscape is carried across the back of the stage opposite to the direction the cart is going. Thus an illusion of progress is created. Even a fireman who actually drinks beer should not present insurmountable problems by now. This, by the way, was one of Rolf Trexler's tricks, he cleverly collected the liquid in a rubber bag backstage after it had run through the puppet.

CHAPTER VIII

Animals

Animal puppets in a theatre ensemble are always very popular with audiences, especially when they take on human characteristics. Before I started to write this book I had given very little thought to animal puppets, and most of the information given in this chapter is derived from the work of other puppeteers. In particular I have used Fedotov's excellent book about techniques in the puppet theatre, 'Technik des Puppentheaters'[1]. My other source of information is Dr. Purschke's magazine 'Perlicko-Perlacko'[2] in which articles by Frantisek Tvrdek, K. Langer, J. Majerova, K. Hlavaty, Vaclav Havlik, Dr. Ladislav Cernak and Dr. Jan Malik on the subject of puppet animals have been published. Actually they originally appeared in the unique and unsurpassed Czech puppet magazine 'Ceskoslovensky Loutkar' which was translated into English by Dr. Pruschke.

As there is a lot of needlework involved in making animal puppets, and as I know very little about needlework, I propose to deal with the subject only in general terms. I hope that my reader will accept this attitude.

As with ordinary puppets the animal's head and limbs are often made of wood or by covering a plasticine model with paper or sacking and glue. Nor is the manipulation — apart from a few particular cases — essentially different from that which we have learnt so far.

Only birds and insects which are to fly through the air have to have a more elaborate system of control. They have to be half glove, half string puppet, that is to say that as long as the bird, for instance, sits in a tree or on the stage it is operated like a glove puppet from below. As soon as it starts to fly, however, a puppeteer on the marionette bridge has to take over the manipulation with a string control. This method not only requires two puppeteers, but also a bridge structure above the glove puppet booth. Usually only very big and well equipped theatres with plenty of operators use this kind of puppet. Small theatres — amateur or professional — usually cannot provide the conditions necessary to the use of different puppet media such as string, rod, glove and shadow puppetry, let alone the black theatre technique. And, moreover we must not forget that extensive technical possibilities are not necessarily a guarantee of artistic quality.

Small birds and insects, by the way, can be very creditably flown through the air with hat elastic on pliable rods which are worked from below, thus avoiding the necessity of using any superstructure.

But let us start with animals' heads. All fifteen of the different drawings in fig. 227 are based on a spherical shape in keeping with a principle adopted by the makers of film cartoon (I think it was Walt Disney who first used the idea in his Mickey Mouse pictures).

To analyse and understand the principle one could imagine the spherical shape to be a geographer's globe mounted on an axis through north and south poles and marked with lines of longitude and latitude. These lines could then be used for the allocation of eye, mouth and nose positions. From a draughtsman's point of vantage each required view, no matter from which angle, can then be easily diagrammatically constructed. As the sphere moves, its silhouette remains unchanged, while the features added seem to move over it keeping their fixed relative positions intact. This idea properly understood makes the three-dimensional aspect of a head easier to envisage.

Without the use of this principle I do not think that the technical perfection of any cartoons, and of Disney's in particular, could ever have been achieved.

Using a sphere as the basic element when drawing animal heads also makes the puppet designer's job very much easier as in this way he can concentrate on the features protruding from the sphere and on their proportions.

We have already said how important the nose is to the 'human' puppet face. This is even more true of the snouts and beaks of animals. The longer a beak, for instance, the wider the circle that is described when the bird moves its head. In such a case even the smallest head movement changes the bird's expression considerably.

---

[1] Published by Friedrich Hofmeister Verlag, VEB, Eastern Germany.
[2] Translated and published by Dr. H. R. Purschke, Hadrianstrasse 3, Frankfurt Main, West Germany.

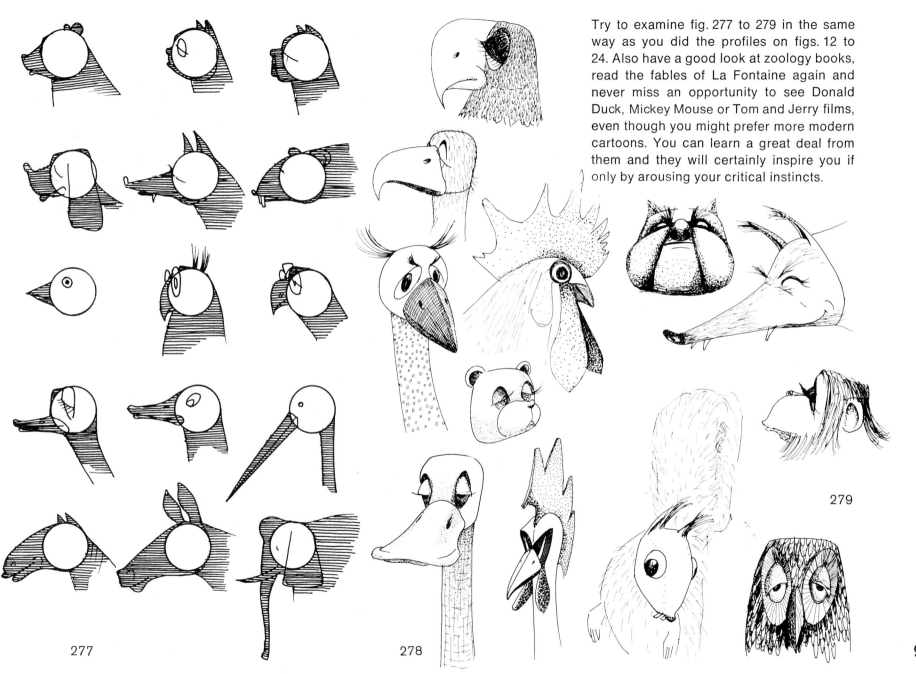

Try to examine fig. 277 to 279 in the same way as you did the profiles on figs. 12 to 24. Also have a good look at zoology books, read the fables of La Fontaine again and never miss an opportunity to see Donald Duck, Mickey Mouse or Tom and Jerry films, even though you might prefer more modern cartoons. You can learn a great deal from them and they will certainly inspire you if only by arousing your critical instincts.

277

278

279

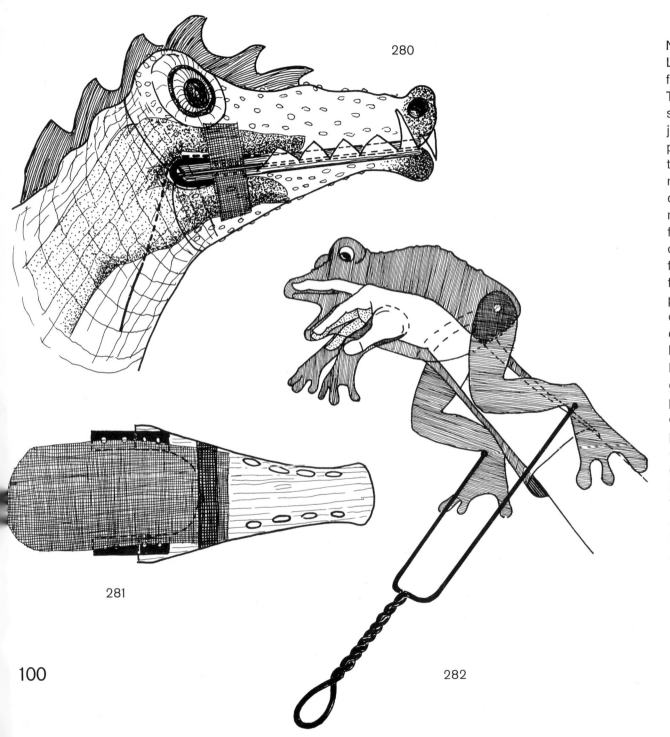

280

281

282

Now to the mechanics of animal puppets. Let us start with the well known crocodile from the puppet theatre of our childhood. Two appropriately shaped pieces of wood serve as upper and lower jaw. They are jointed together either with two strong pieces of leather or with two hinges. The two U-shaped parts in fig. 281 (dotted line) make up the throat which is lined with red cloth. This is only fastened to the roof of the mouth of the crocodile and hangs down in front of the puppeteer's hands (compare dotted line on fig. 280 and shaded part on fig. 281). Leather loops for the puppeteer's fingers in both upper and lower jaw complete the mechanical requirement of the crocodile head. Its teeth fit either into holes cut into the opposite jaw or into the gaps between the opposite teeth.

If the U-shaped parts are made large enough, the crocodile can actually 'eat' his prey. His head can be made by covering a clay, plasticine or polystyrene model with paper and glue, or, of course of cloth padded with cotton wool. It is also quite easy to give him movable eyes and to lead tubes to his nostrils for smoke.

The very simple and practical flap mechanism devised for the crocodile's mouth can be used successfully for almost any animal, and is also particularly effective for birds' beaks. A simple cloth tube is sufficient for a body.

Fedotov's frog in fig. 282 has a stiff head and body; only the lower jaw and the legs are movable. Head and body are most conveniently made by covering a model with paper and glue. The front legs are made of cloth and they are operated like the arms of an ordinary glove puppet with thumb and little finger.

The hind legs have three joints each and are manipulated with the aid of a simple wire fork. A piece of elastic could be led inside the legs through to the body to pull the legs back into their normal position after each jump. Like the front legs, the hind legs are also best made of stuffed cloth tubes as these will not make any unwanted noise. A small dog could easily be made after the same principle. But if you want to make a bigger dog, and especially if you want him to wag his tail it would be best to give him a rigid head and a rigid behind as seen on fig. 283. For a sure grip, it is advisable to fasten a loop for the fingers inside the back part. Thumb and index finger wag the tail. Lower jaw and ears can be manipulated with three fingers as shown in fig. 283. This kind of dog seems to portray the funny movements typical of a boxer puppy quite well. Vaclav Havlik thought of an excellent mechanism for imitating the movement of a cantering horse, greyhound, or hare. Figs. 284 A and 284 B show the full extent of the movement that can be achieved by a puppet made according to his design.

Three appropriate pieces of plywood form the basic structure of the body. Glue blocks of polystyrene on to both sides of the plywood and carve them into shape with file, rasp and sandpaper or with a hot blade or wire. Special electric tools for working in polystyrene can be bought relatively cheaply from craftwork shops. Cover the polystyrene shapes with paper and glue to make

them robust and strong. Head and body parts are connected with strong steel springs. Spring blades are better than spiral springs, but the latter are easier to get. The manipulation rod which is rounded and spreads at the top is then fastened to the spring that connects the chest and hip sections of the body. Two flat metal plates screwed to the sides of the top of the manipulation rod guard the spring and stop it from twisting unexpectedly out of alignment. These plates should give adequate side cover to the springs; I have not included them in the drawing as, if I did so, the clarity of the design would be impaired. When all is ready cover the gaps between the three parts with cloth and fix the legs firmly to the body. Balance the body properly and then connect chest and rear part to the manipulation ring on the rod with the necessary lengths of wire, as seen in fig. 284 A. The sliding manipulation ring should have a groove for the puppeteer's fingers or an area of matt surface for grip.

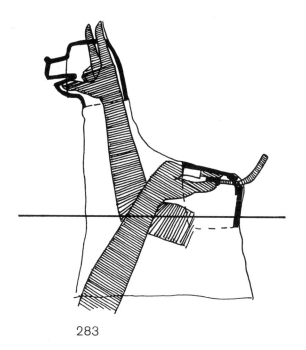

283

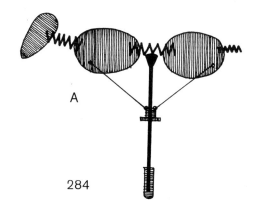

A

284

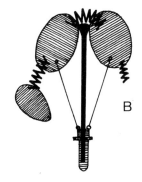

B

285

286

287

288

289

102

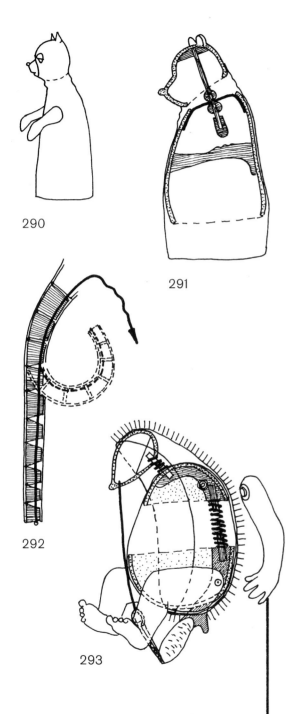

290

291

292

293

This sort of mechanism is particularly suitable when depicting the famous race between hedgehog and hare, for instance. But as soon as the hare stops running and starts to talk to the hedgehog, the audience expects the hare to sit up, an action which a puppet with this kind of mechanism cannot do very convincingly. Therefore it is best to have a second hare with identical looks, but a different mechanism, and which can, at given points, be exchanged for the galloping hare. The director of such a scene can decide whether he should have the second hare made like an ordinary glove puppet or like the owl shown in fig. 285 or the bear in fig. 291. Needless to say, to be convincing both hares should look very much alike.

After having dealt very thoroughly with this type of puppet it seems unnecessary to go into any further explanation of fig. 285 to 291.

The elephant's trunk in 292 is made from a tapered cardboard tube, which is cut as shown in the drawing. The white gussets shown on the drawing are the parts cut away. The individual pieces are then connected together by a strip of cloth glued along the front of the trunk. The whole trunk is then covered with a cloth tube which is best glued to it at the top and at the bottom to prevent it from twisting or slipping around the cardboard structure. A string fastened to the tip of the trunk and running through it when pulled from a point inside the body will make the trunk curl. This is another of Fedotov's inventions.

The hedgehog that curls itself into a ball in fig. 293 was made by Vaclav Havlik. For a puppet of this type, head and body are made from egg-shaped models covered with paper and glue. Once the paper mould is dry the body is cut in two about one third of the way from the lower end, and a mechanism is built inside it. As shown in the diagram the chest and the lower part of the body are far enough apart not to touch when the hedgehog curls up. The back of head and body are covered with a 'hood' of foam rubber 1 cm thick which has been provided with bristles. The foam rubber is let in to give it the desired shape.

For the bristles you can use nylon string, raffia, wool or paper string. A good way to get an even length for each bristle is to wind whatever material you are using round a ruler or a piece of plywood corresponding in width to the desired length of the bristles. If you then cut the material along one edge of the ruler, you get double length bristles. By threading each double length through the foam rubber hood (not in straight lines!) and tying it with a knot, an even lot of bristles is firmly attached to it. There is one snag, however, and that is that foam rubber is not a very strong material. It might, therefore, be better to thread the double bristle, through the foam rubber with a curved needle and secure it with a dab of Bostik from the inside rather than tie a knot which might tear loose from the foam Havlik suggests cutting a template edged with a wavy line and using this to incise the foam rubber at intervals across. The bristles are then planted into these incisions. Two advantages of this method are claimed, the foam is more flexible and the bristles show

103

a pleasing natural irregularity. Very skilful people, I suppose, can do this, but the foam need only be cut too deeply in one place for the whole coat to be ruined. Quite apart from this the grooving process must weaken the foam rubber very considerably.

The arms of Havlik's hedgehod are fixed to its body with strong press-studs. This is an excellent idea, as during the performance an arm can quickly and easily be exchanged for one holding a pipe or a newspaper as the script may require.

The construction of the fighting bull on fig. 294 is based on the principle of the umbrella. This is a simple principle and has often been used for both puppets and props. A metal tube is slipped over a manipulation rod which has a handle at its lower end. The metal plates to which the joints for the two stays are fastened are welded to the metal tube. The stays are connected flexibly to the wooden spine of the bull. A strong, well chosen spiral spring pushes the spine into its normal (straight) position indicated by the dotted line on fig. 294. By pushing the metal tube downwards the spring compresses and the bull's back bends. Letting the tube go releases the spring and pushes the animal's back straight again.

A very strong thick piece of rubber which can be covered with starched linen serves as the basic support for the bull's neck. The thickness of the rubber is chosen according to its desired flexibility. The thinner it is the easier it is to bend in any direction and, in order to limit this tendency, a few thin strips of wood should be screwed to both sides of the rubber at regular intervals. These strips, while giving it support will not interfere with the side to side movement of the neck. Two strong pieces of plywood — also screwed to the rubber — form the bearing for the nodding action of the head. Head and body are conveniently made by covering a model with paper and glue. An alternative way of making the body could be to use wire hoops and sew the bull's coat onto them.

The drawings in figs. 295, 296 and 297 show pretty accurately the construction of Havlik's fox, the only difference from the original being the fact that it had two pieces for the body (chest and lower section) instead of one as in my drawings. Chest and lower piece were connected with a strong spring, which, of course, made the fox's body more supple. Havlik's idea was to combine the horizontal running action and the vertical sitting-up action previously discussed in connection with the hare. By combining both actions in one puppet, he managed to do without a second puppet. The cross-section in 295 illustrates the basic idea. The body consists of different materials. There is wood for the back and for the bearings which support the legs. There are 2 plywood pieces and some polystyrene and paper moulding. Constructed in the manner shown, the fox's belly has a slot into which the central manipulation rod can disappear when the fox sits up, as the rod moves in one direction only, (compare fig. 296). If the fox's coat is arranged cleverly, neither slot nor rod should be seen by members of the audience, even if the fox turns his belly straight to them when sitting up. For reasons of clarity fig. 295 is not to scale; slot and body width are not in correct proportion to one another.

The neck is also made of a spiral spring. In order to give the spring strength and prevent it from squeaking, it is covered with rubber or plastic tubing. Tail and body are likewise connected by springs. In order to control the tail with a manipulation rod, Havlik drilled a hole of the same diameter as the tail spring through a wooden ball. One end of the spring is fastened to the fox's rump, the other end is pushed through the ball and fastened to it. The manipulating rod is then fastened to the ball.

The head is manipulated by two thin steel rods which are fixed loosely to each temple of the animal. Both rods are inserted at an angle and fixed into a wooden cube. This cube is used as a handle. From the lower jaw a nylon string runs down through a hole in the same cube. A wooden bead tied to the end of the nylon string stops it from slipping out of the hole, and makes it easy to pull. An elastic band fastened between the jaws pulls the lower jaw shut.

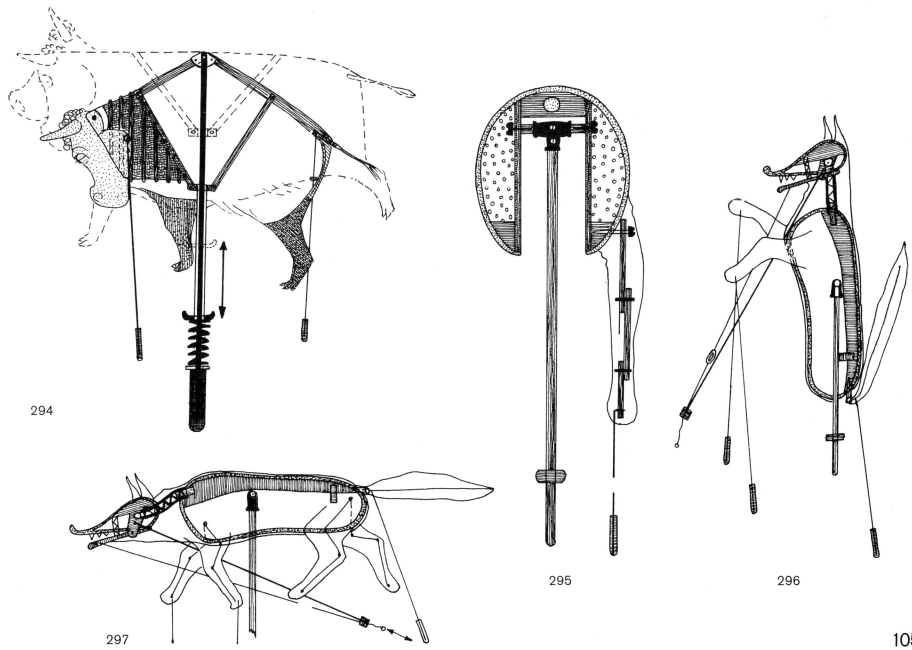

294

295

296

297

105

Now, as we approach the end of this chapter, I would like to describe a construction devised to enable one operator to work a coach with horse and driver. But before I begin I must inform you that such a piece of apparatus is cumbersome and heavy, and its use would only be justified and practicable in a large and well staffed professional theatre, or in a play that revolves solely around such a coach. In the latter case the coach could be stationary with wheels turning and horse appearing to walk or gallop while the scenery could pass behind to give the illusion of progressive movement. The scenery could either be carried piecemeal by puppeteers, or fixed to a moving conveyor belt or a revolving stage. Another method would be to project moving pictures (representing passing scenery) on to a screen behind the coach, and yet another idea would be to work in a round theatre with a stage going round the auditorium, the audience sitting in the middle. But in Germany, and I imagine in most countries, such sophisticated working conditions would be considered completely utopian, and I quote these few suggestions in order to indicate the magnitude of the subject. A whole book could be written on puppet theatre props and staging facilities alone.

But to return to the coach and horse, the shaded area in fig. 298 represents a piece of plywood supporting the top of the carriage, the fork-shaped carriage shafts, together with the horse and the wheels with their bearings and cranks. As the vehicle is very heavy, and as the puppeteer needs both hands for setting it in motion, the weight must be either supported by a rolling device beneath the actual playboard, or by a stand on wheels which can be wheeled along the stage-floor. Both methods guarantee that the coach appears to be driving along easily on the level.

At the point of its centre of gravity the horse is mounted on a fulcrum — between the two shafts. The front axle of the carriage is made of a strong iron bar or pipe. This bar does not go straight from one wheel to the other, but has a U-shaped bend near the plywood support (compare fig. 222) so that it can be used as a crank-shaft for the connecting rod which activates the leg-moving device. This device consists of two Z-shaped structures, each made of 3 pieces of wood loosely jointed together. The centre points of each Z-structure are firmly interconnected by the axle which is also the horse's fulcrum. The connecting rod from the front wheel axle crank is jointed to the rear (or top) elbow of the nearside Z-structure, the free ends of which are jointed to the top of the nearside fore-leg, and to a point below the axis of the nearside hind-leg. With the far-side Z-structure the joint to the fore-leg is made below the leg axle and to the hind-leg at a point above the axle. The far-side Z-pieces can be seen to be slightly longer than the nearside ones for obvious reasons. This arrangement if carefully proportioned gives the animal the correct horse's gait and not a 'camel walk'.

As the fore and aft carriage wheels are of different sizes, they will need different ratio pulleys to drive them in order to get a realistic relative speed effect. The transmission from the crank pulleys to the wheel pulleys is best done with strong rubber bands. From the joint where the leg-activating connecting rod is attached to the Z-joint, another connecting rod goes to the head of the horse. This rod makes the horse's head nod in time to the walking action. The horse's neck and head are loosely jointed together, and the neck can be constructed in the same way as that of the bull described earlier.

The coachman is firmly fixed to his seat and can be operated from inside the coach with the help of a suitable control. The drawing in fig. 298 shows the lower part of the inside of the carriage separated into two halves. But I am sure this could be avoided with a little thoughtful planning.

In conclusion I should say that only someone with considerable woodworking and mechanical experience should attempt to make the structure I have described, and before embarking on a major venture such as this it would definitely be advisable to try out the mechanics on a model.

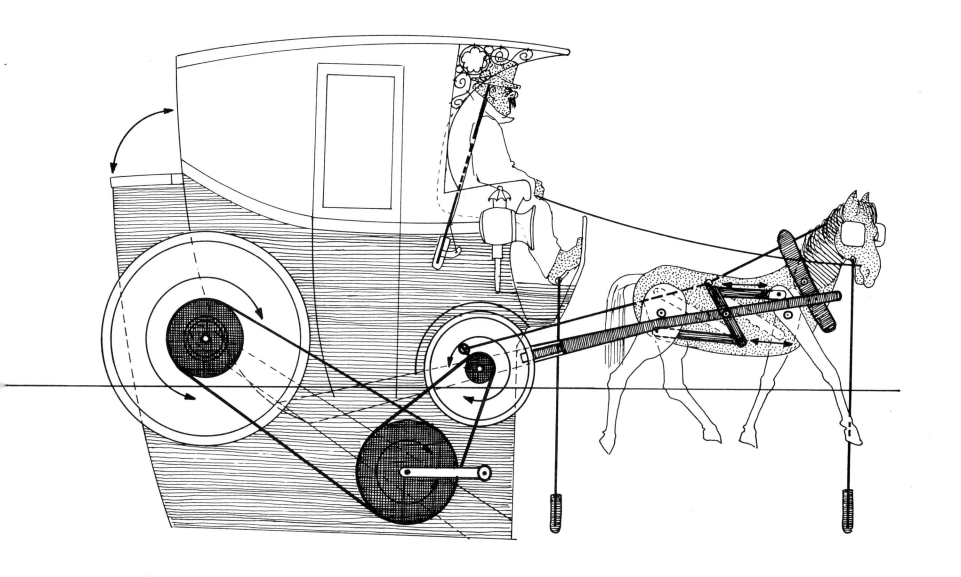

CHAPTER IX

Puppet Clothes and Costumes

Before I go on to discuss puppet costumes and their patterns I feel the necessity to stress again the difference between a puppet and a doll, a difference that extends, of course, to the ways in which they are dressed. Usually a doll belongs to a child by whom it is dressed and undressed. Anybody can look at it, touch it and handle it, and it is often displayed in the nursery for decorative purposes. A doll, usually, cannot move by itself unless it has some built-in mechanism. But this to my way of thinking destroys the very element which brings a doll to life, namely the child's imagination. In a doll the child finds a companion with whom it can identify, and it stands to reason, therefore, that the most sought after dolls are the nice looking ones.

The puppet, however, has a totally different purpose and field of action. It is a symbol for a person or an animal and it only comes to life in the hands of a skilful puppeteer during a performance. It is not touched or handled by the audience, but is observed from a distance. So the puppet's costume has no other function but to assist in the definition of the character by means of colour, form and structure. The purpose of the puppet costume is to create an illusion. It need not be complete, nor need it be removable as is the dress of a doll or of a human. The puppet costume should in no way impede the puppet's movement, but should rather help to accentuate it. There is no need for a puppet pocket to really function as a pocket, nor is there any need for silk linings, heavy solid gilded crowns or braided seams. All these, more likely than not, will stand in the way of a puppet's movement. The true value of a puppet is judged by the visual effect which it creates and not by the costliness of the material in which it is clad. A puppet is usually a quarter or a fifth of the size of a human. Theoretically this means that the materials used for puppet costumes should be four or five times thinner and more supple than those used for human costumes, so that a corresponding degree of flowing movement and authentic shape, can be represented.

In practice this is only possible to a very limited degree and a seamstress making a puppet costume must use every known device to avoid stiffness and weight in the finished garment. She would, for instance, decorate the collar of a puppet costume with gold paint rather than with gold braid. Or if the puppet's shirt is only to be seen from the front, she would make not a complete shirt, but only a 'bib' and this she would either glue to the puppet's chest, or sew to the inside of its jacket. As said before, it is the illusion that counts where puppet costume is concerned.

For our purposes old pieces of material from shirts, dresses and linings are preferable to new, starched cloths. It is usually worth one's while to dye silk or muslin or to decorate it with batik in order to obtain the most suitable results in colour and pattern. Or if you need a costume with a special design, you can simply paint it on to plain material. For a knight's coat of mail, sacking can be sprayed with bronze or silver spray and it will be found that, with a bit of clever lighting, the illusion of iron or bronze chainmail is complete. Again, it is not the material itself that matters, so much as the illusion it creates.

Right from the start the effect of stage lighting should be considered when selecting paints and deciding on the colours of costume materials, and it is therefore advisable to look at the proposed colours and material under the conditions of lighting which will ultimately be used during performance. All puppets should have a certain uniformity of style and a carefully considered colour scheme.

As well as providing a scene with visual enhancement a set should always have interesting possibilities for the puppet actors' entrances and exits and their movements on stage. It should, of course, also conjure up the apppropriate atmosphere for the puppet play's environment. If a set does not fulfil these three requirements it is superfluous. Even if a set is an excellent design in its own right, with perfect composition and colouring it must be regarded as a failure, if it encroaches on the effectivity of the puppets on stage.

Therefore the shapes and colours of a set should be kept as simple and unobtrusive as possible. The shapes and colours of puppets and their costumes should always be clearer, brighter and stronger than those of the sets in which they appear. A most effective combination would, for instance, be a stylised set in varying shades of grey with clear-cut and colourful puppets. With coloured stage lighting one could then brighten up or darken or even tint certain areas of the set, as might be appropriate.

In fig. 299 the most basic costume patterns are drawn on graph paper. If you enlarge these patterns five times you will have the correct size pattern for a normal puppet.

Here is a list of the items illustrated in fig. 299.

A Basic pattern for a plain under-garment made from calico or any other material. It can also be the back of a long coat.

B Straight front piece of a jacket — or, fitting to back A, a coat if lengthened accordingly.

C Rounded off front piece of a jacket.

D Sleeve for under-garment, coat or jacket.

E Back for B or C.

F Collar.

G Back of a tailcoat.

H Tails for G.

J Front part of a tail coat. (This could also be cut straight.)

K Pattern for trousers or a woman's skirt.

With costumes that consist of shirt, trousers, and jacket combined it is advisable to fix the trousers to a sleeveless under-garment because if they are fastened directly to the jacket, they cannot move freely when the puppet turns, bends, or stoops.

The elementary garments suggested here are not particularly effective in themselves, but step by step you will learn to make them more effective. Experiment with various paper patterns by sticking them to the puppet you are working on before cutting the actual material you are to use.

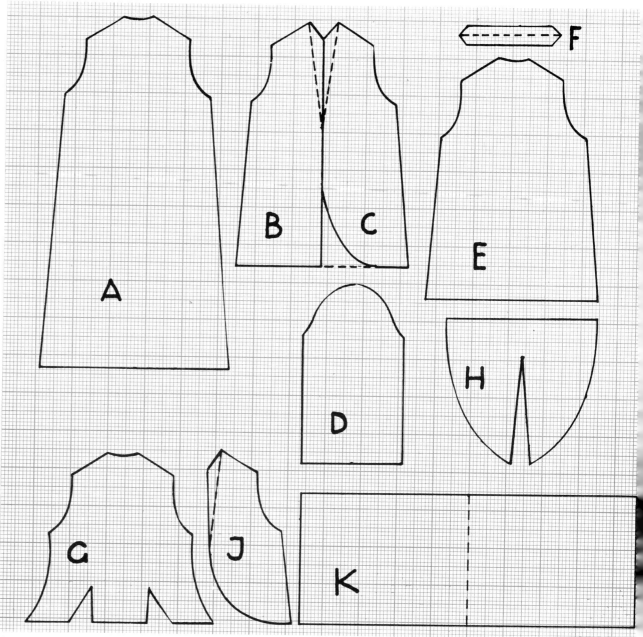

299

Figs. 300-303 show some ordinary European garments.

A stands for front
B stands for back
C stands for sleeve
D stands for collar
E stands for pocket

Next to each pattern you have a drawing of the finished garment. The black gussets indicate where the material has to be taken in. If you know little or nothing about sewing, it might be an idea to take an old garment of yours to pieces and examine how it was made.

So far we have only dealt with ordinary European dress. For something more fanciful and exotic we usually turn to clothing traditions from other parts of the world. You will be amazed to find that some of the most beautiful old costumes have very simple patterns, being usually based on simple geometrical shapes, such as squares, rectangles, trapezoids, triangles and circles, and that they are sometimes cut from a single piece of material.

The Japanese kimono, for instance, is one of the simplest and at the same time most beautiful garments in the world. Its beauty probably stems from the combination of its simple geometrical pattern and its tastefully subdued colours. In fig. 304 there are three kimono models for men (shaded), and one with a floral pattern for women. For the latter elongated sleeves, which are also used as pockets, are typical. Part of a lady's kimono is a broad cloth belt called an 'obi' which gathers the garment between hip and breast and is skilfully tied in a knot at the

110

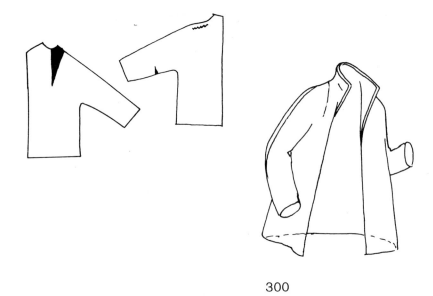

300

301

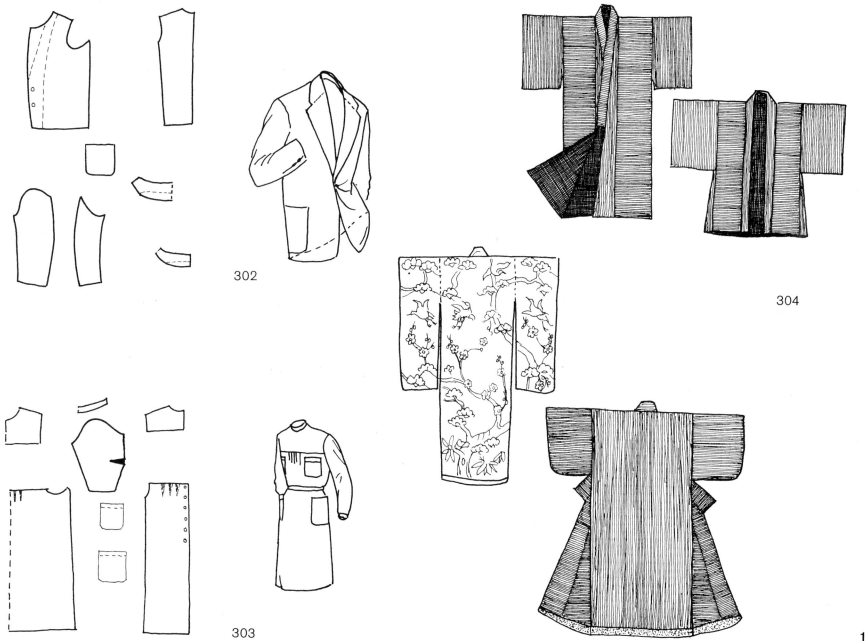

302

303

304

back (see fig. 315). A kimono is always made according to the same pattern. It is composed of several rectangular pieces of cloth. I have shaded the different pieces on the drawings in different ways to make this quite clear. Rather more elaborate is the festive kimono of an actor as seen in the lower drawing of the mens' kimonos.

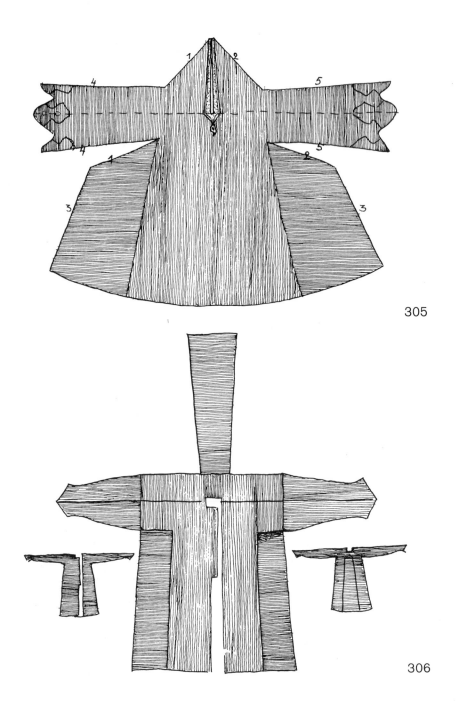

305

The Persian felt coat is made of a single piece of material as shown in fig. 305. The lines on the drawing do not represent seams, but indicate points at which the material is folded round or sewn together. If you could imagine a person to be wearing the coat, his head would seem to stick out above the dotted horizontal line. The chest triangle and half the sleeve hang down and are sewn to the front pieces. All edges with identical numbers are sewn together. The slot for the neck and the cuffs are decorated with embroidery.

The garment shown in fig. 306 is also of Persian origin. The large drawing in the middle shows the complete pattern, which is composed of several parts as indicated. The small drawing on the left shows the front view, the one on the right the back view of the garment.

112

306

Equally simple are the patterns of North African, Tunisian and Algerian garments. The striped 'burnous', fig. 307, is made of a single piece of coarse woollen cloth and forms the popular hooded cloak of the Islamic peasants. The festive, square, two-coloured garment for men (308) is very simple to make. The hole for the head, the slit down the front, the top of the sleeves and the holes for the hands are decorated with embroidered ribbon.

In 309 can be seen a waistcoat made of cloth with buttons along one shoulder. This is called a 'firmla'. I have not included the typical North African trousers that go with it as they are very simple to make from two rectangular pieces of cloth which are about two and a half times as wide as the length of the leg. They have a slit at the outside corners for the feet. At the waist they are held together with a knitted woollen cord.

The colourful, festive Jewish dress from Tripolis is composed of squares and triangles only. A bodice or waistcoat is usually worn over it.

Fig. 311 shows the so-called 'casabia', the common garment of craftsmen, shopkeepers and camel drivers. It is usually made of grey, white, or brown coarse 'Haik' material (compare 313) and decorated at the seams with white woollen braid.

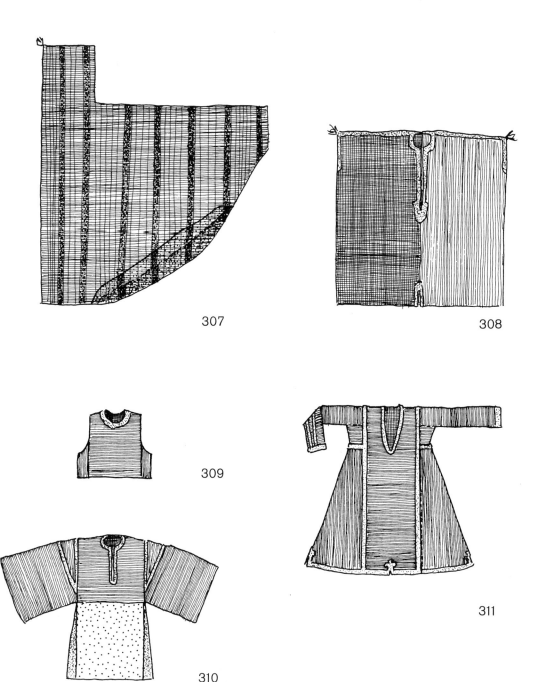

307

308

309

310

311

Very picturesque and interesting is the headgear of the Islamic people, see figure 312 a-k:

a 'Okal', a double ring for the head to keep in place the scarf which protects head and neck.

b 'Koffia' or 'keffijeh', the scarf protecting head and neck along with the 'okal'.

c and d Felt caps worn by Dervishes.

e Padded headgear of green material. This supports the turban scarf making the turban appear impressively large.

f Decorated cap.

g Dervish headgear made with two layers of felt.

h Headgear with turban worn by the door-keeper of the mosque at Jerusalem. The main part of the headgear has red and green stripes and the scarf is green.

i High cap with turban scarf, over the scarf a fez and to the side a tarboosh.

k 'Fez', the most popular Turkish headgear.

114

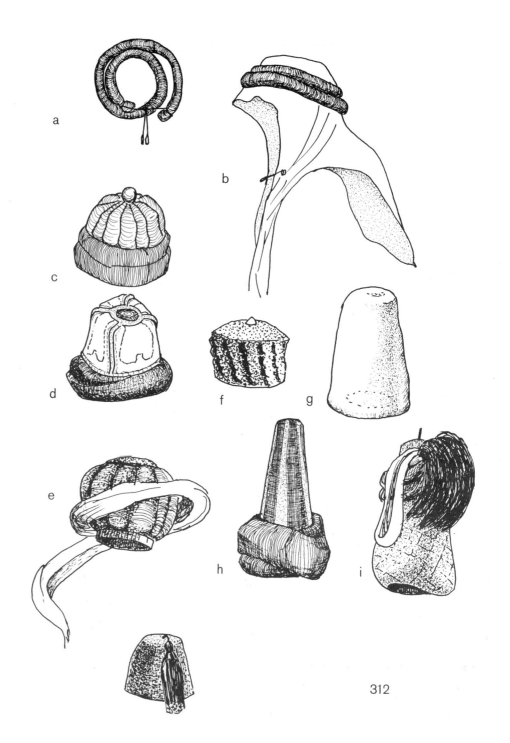

312

Figs. 313 and 314 show a 'haik' seen from three different sides. From the small drawing below it can be seen that the 'haik' has a semi-circular pattern. The little ribbon (314) shows how the 'haik' is worn which, incidentally, is the way in which the Romans wore their 'togas'. As you can see it is fastened to the under-garment on the left side of the chest.

A Japanese friend of mine gave me the little doll shown in fig. 315. She is wearing — so I was told — a widow's costume made of dark red matt silk with a gold pattern woven into it. From the knee downwards the colour changes gradually to black. The collar is also made of black material. Underneath this kimono she wears a white one which can be seen at the collar. The broad belt or 'obi' is made of black silk with a gold pattern. The ingenious bow at the back is held together by a plaited cord. Japanese ladies are said to sleep with their heads on wooden headrests in order to preserve their magnificent coiffures, although their hair is only dressed in this way on festive occasions.

313

314

315

115

As we draw towards the end of our journey into the realm of the puppetmaker, let us examine a few examples of historical European fashion. I refer, as before, to the excellent and well known book on costumes by Max Tilke 'Kostümschnitte und Gewandformen'[1] which every serious puppetmaker should know.

Here are some examples of Spanish fashion as worn in Germany and Holland in the 17th century (these are from the Historical Museum in Dresden):

316 Royal garment of Christian II made of blue silk embroidered with gold thread with collar made of velvet.

317 Wedding attire of Johann Georg I, Kurfürst of Saxony (1611-1656). The coat is made of black velvet richly embroidered with gold thread.

318 Hat of Christian II (1604) made of sea green satin with rich silk embroidery.

319 Hat and wig of a Dutch courtier.

320 and 321 Two silk court dresses decorated with gold braid (1650-1680).

322 Coat of Dutch courtier (1630-1640) very similar in pattern to the latter baroque style (this is also true of their wigs and hats).

323 Simple Renaissance collar with the pattern based on a square folded once and worn as indicated in the three small drawings of fig. 323.

324 Circular cloak of Christian II made of blue satin with silk embroidery. The embroidery depicts the river Elbe with all her towns.

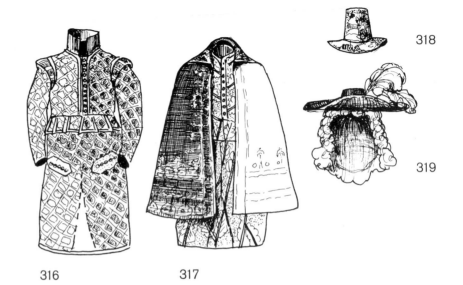

316   317   318   319

320

321

[1] Published by Verlag Ernst Wasmuth, Tubingen.

And here are a few examples from the Baroque and Roccoco fashions of the 18th century up to the French Revolution.

The 18th century in Europe was the age of subtlety and artificiality. People behaved and dressed theatrically — hence the extraordinary fashions current amongst the nobility and the rich bourgeoisie of that time. Patterns for garments have never since been so complicated and intricate.

325 A courtier's long jacket made of no less than 16 parts, not counting buttons trimming and lace.

326 Jacket made of fewer parts than in 325, yet still of a very extravagant and complicated cut. No pleats, but rich gold and silver braiding down the front.

327 Fashions of the age demanded severe sacrifices on the part of women, who were preferred voluptuous and fullbosomed, but were expected to have absurdly slim waists. To achieve this women were pressed into corsets stiffened by whale-bone stays.

328 The crinoline was a special feature of the time. It was a kind of inverted basket fastened to the lower part of the corset and it served as an extension to womens' hips and posteriors. The dress was skilfully arranged over it.

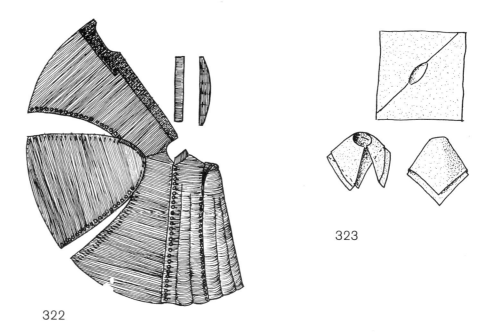

323

322

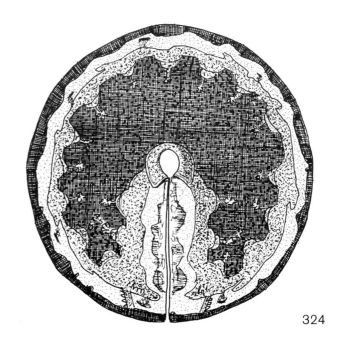

324

117

329 At that time gentlemen wore wigs which could be taken off — to the great surprise, I suppose, of the American Red Indians whose great idea was to scalp their would-be conquerors. Fig. 329 shows a Prussian wig and plait, a rather austere type of wig for those days.

On top of the wig a three-cornered hat was worn. At three points the broad brim was fastened to the crown of the hat. Especially elaborate ones were decorated with lace. The famous French full-bottomed wig was much longer and fuller and was continually being powdered. To fight the lice which used to find a comfortable home under wigs, people used wooden or ivory sticks with little scratching hands at the end.

But I am supposed to be writing a book of instructions for puppet makers and not a study of cultural and social history, so I shall stop here.

I am sure that several problems discussed in this book could be solved differently from the way in which I have suggested. Also I feel strongly that much remains to be said about staging, sets, black theatre, manipulation of puppets and directing of puppet shows, but all of these I could only mention in passing and not fully deal with here.

In spite of this I hope that I have been a source of inspiration to both the beginner and the more advanced puppet maker and that they will be encouraged to venture into ever more interesting work. In this way I trust that this book may prove to be of some service to all those who love puppetry.

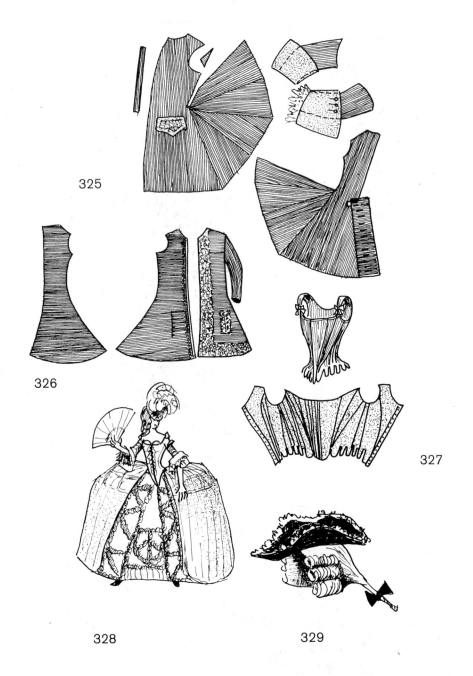

325

326

327

328

329